Journeys Toward Home

Printed in the United States of America
ISBN: 978-0-9863992-7-5
Library of Congress Control Number: 2024924608

Writers Bloc
Jonesboro, Arkansas

Journeys Toward Home

Essays on Ancestors and their Paths to Missouri

BY RUTH WEHMER HAWKINS

For the generations that came before me

Contents

Notes

A book that draws heavily on genealogical research is not ever finished. New discoveries await, such as documents and photographs in strange places and previously unknown relatives with family information. This book is a result of 25 years of sporadic research and development that will continue.

One difficulty in researching ancestors is that consistent spelling of names did not become important until the late 19th century. I have attempted some standardization by using the most common spellings before and after they came to America. To further complicate research, state borders and county lines shifted over time, making it appear that some families lived in several places, though they remained in the same spot. Because these essays are meant for a general audience, I have shortened many footnotes. However, they contain enough information to locate sources.

Additionally, instead of a general index at the end, a family direct line chart follows each essay, including dates and locations of births, marriages and deaths. Charts generally begin with the immigrant ancestor and show direct lines to James Henry Wehmer or Hazel Marie Snoddy, the last generation in these essays.

I have chosen to focus on direct ancestors, but my research includes extended families to varying degrees. Those who wish to know more about ancestors not included, or who have additional information or corrections on individuals in these essays, may contact me via email.

RuthHawkins1965@gmail.com.

Acknowledgments

This book of essays would never have become reality without encouragement and support from my husband and primary editor Van Hawkins. His keen eye, astute observations and judicious cuts made this a better book.

I owe a special debt of gratitude to my cousin Lou Wehmer who got me started on family genealogy when he shared a copy of his early family research, conducted largely at German archives and records repositories. Other cousins enhanced this book by recounting memories passed down from their parents, as well as their own recollections. Significant contributions came from Susan Wehmer Kagy, Virginia Wehmer Borcherding, Barbara Wehmer Skaggs, Norman Wehmer, Alex and Mary Fife, Mary Fife Powell and Ross Maxwell. Over the years my 11 siblings helped me by recalling memories of our parents and stories of growing up on Old Jamestown Road in Florissant. Their names appear in the James and Hazel Wehmer family tree included in this book. My son and daughter-in-law, Curt Hawkins and Amy Schmidt, read final drafts of the essays to catch errors.

I have attempted to use original sources throughout my research, but several well-documented histories on early family lines included in these essays have pointed me in the right directions to find these sources. Repositories and online databases also have been invaluable in locating facsimiles of original documents. Classes through the International Institute of Genealogical Studies gave focus to my efforts and helped me organize genealogical materials and research.

Finally, special thanks to Mary Melton of Jonesboro, Arkansas, for her assistance in enhancing historic maps and to Notley Hawkins of Columbia, Missouri, for capturing striking photographic images of two Fife oil portraits from the 19th century.

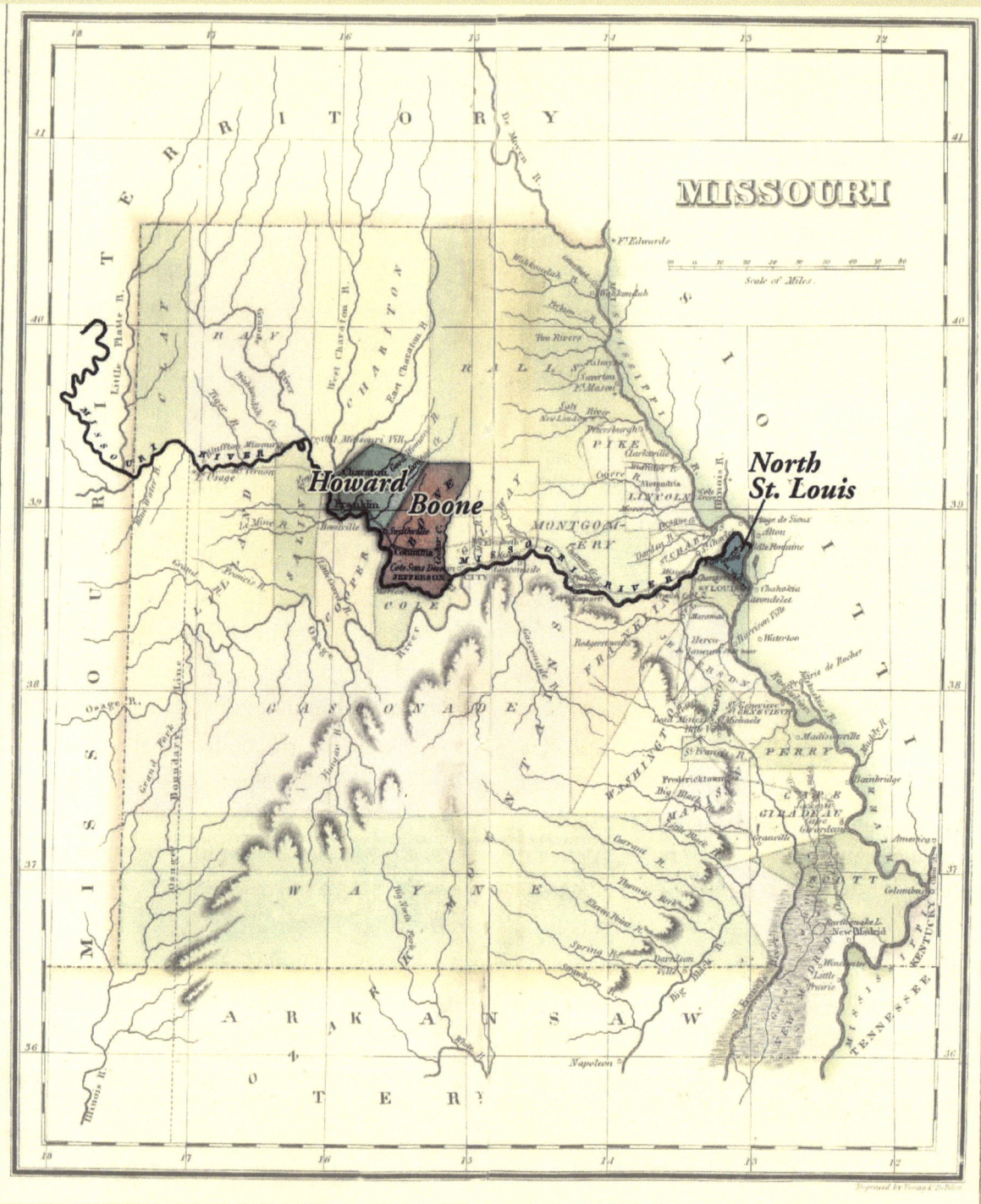

1827 map of Missouri engraved by Young & Delleker. Ancestors of James H. Wehmer and Hazel Marie Snoddy ultimately settled along the Missouri River in Boone, Howard and St. Louis counties. (Map Collection, State Historical Society of Missouri)

Introduction

To appreciate our ancestors, one must understand the times and places in which they lived and events and experiences that shaped their lives. We must know about their struggles and recognize how much is owed to the perseverance and sacrifices of generations that came before us. These are stories of my family, embedded in history to comprehend their passages.

Essays herein focus on my grandparents' paternal and maternal family lines: Riggs, Snoddy, Denny, Fife, Carrico, Thompson, Wehmer and Buhrmester. They lived through waves of European immigration, the American Revolutionary War, Indian Wars, the War of 1812, the Louisiana Purchase, America's Civil War, a Great Depression, World Wars I and II and other important historical events.

This saga follows only direct ancestors of my parents, James Henry Wehmer and Hazel Marie Snoddy, singling out some who are representative of hardships faced by all. It does not include other branches of each family line that may have had different experiences.

Essays in Part One begin with the earliest family line to arrive in America (Riggs) and end with the last to immigrate (Wehmer and Buhrmester). Some lived in identical places and participated in the same events. No matter when and where their journey began, all eight family lines had one thing in common -- they ended in rural Missouri. Their paths reflect typical westward migration patterns, placing them among thousands of brave souls who traveled similar arduous routes. The earliest family line (Riggs) immigrated from England in 1633 and settled in New England's colonies. When land began losing fertility, they joined settlers following the Great Wagon Road into Maryland, Virginia and North Carolina. Other family lines (Carrico, Snoddy, Denny) immigrated directly to these lower colonies where fertile land remained plentiful.

After the Revolutionary War, our expanding nation acquired territories as far as the Mississippi River, and pioneers pushed westward. Kentucky became a popular destination for trans-Appalachian travelers after Daniel Boone cut a path through Cumberland Gap along the Wilderness Trail. Between 1780 and 1800, four family lines (Riggs, Snoddy, Denny, Carrico) scaled mountains with their meager possessions, crossed through this Gap and settled in Kentucky. A fifth family line (Fife) established roots in Kentucky when a young man from County Tyrone, Northern Ireland, immigrated to Madison County. By the time he arrived, the other four families had moved on to Missouri.

One of them (Carrico) responded to offers of cheap land in Spanish-owned Louisiana Territory around St. Louis. The others (Riggs, Snoddy, Denny) came after the Louisiana Purchase when U. S. land grants became available for War of 1812 service. These families followed Boon's Lick Road, running roughly parallel to the Missouri River, and settled in what became Boone and Howard counties.

Only three lines immigrated directly to St. Louis. The Thompsons arrived in the 1840s, escaping overcrowding and terrible disease that accompanied expanding industrialization in Glasgow, Scotland. They joined other relatives who reached Missouri earlier by coming upriver on the Mississippi from New Orleans, a busy port accepting immigrants. Two other lines (Wehmer, Buhrmester) arrived from Prussia in the 1860s to avoid turmoil in Prussia and other Germanic states. They chose the St. Louis area because many German enclaves already were established there and across the river in Illinois.

Essays in Part Two memorialize my parents and grandparents. Their stories place them within the context of earlier generations and illustrate how ancestors influenced them in subtle and not-so-subtle ways. These families braved tumultuous oceans, rugged mountains, mighty rivers and inhospitable lands to come to Missouri. They did so with indomitable spirits full of hope, courage, (probably with stubbornness, too) and determination to follow their dreams wherever they led them.

Land ownership was almost always a primary goal for early westward movement in the United States. In the 1840s, Manifest Destiny came to represent inevitability of expansion across the continent. Family lines arriving here did not follow others to the Pacific Coast. Instead, they remained in Missouri through the 20th century and into the 21st century. Destiny carried them only so far as the Mississippi and Missouri rivers in what became the State of Missouri in 1821. And there they stayed to live their lives.

Part One

Prayer formed a major part of daily life for Puritans at Massachusetts Bay Colony. Families were the basic unit of society, with husbands required to provide for household needs, protect their families and teach children to live a God-centered life. (Painting by Henry Mosler, 1897, Theodor Horydczak Collection, Library of Congress)

Puritan Exodus from England
Edward Riggs

Englishman Edward Riggs faced two difficult choices in the 1630s. He could change his Puritan beliefs to avoid being thrown into prison, maimed or executed as a heretic. Or he and his family could risk crossing the turbulent Atlantic Ocean with other Puritans to establish a colony where they could worship in their own way. He chose the latter but paid a high price. His wife and three of his five children were dead within 18 months of their arrival.

Since England's break with Catholicism during the 1500s, growing discontent emerged among those who believed the Protestant Reformation remained too Catholic. After unsuccessful efforts to purify the church, a Puritan group known as Pilgrims broke all ties with the Church of England, believing it could never be sufficiently reformed. They sailed from England on *The Mayflower* in 1620 and founded Plymouth Colony in New England to freely practice their religion. Those who remained behind, however, held out hope that the Church of England could be "purified" from within. That proved not to be the case, and hopes faded when King Charles I dissolved Parliament with its growing Puritan majority. Soldiers attempted to root out anyone who disagreed with the king's religious policies, leading to persecution. Vocal critics of the church endured such punishments as imprisonment, cutting off ears, flogging bare backs, dragging behind an oxcart, placing in pillories or branding cheeks with letters "SL" for seditious libeller.[1]

Essex County, and particularly the town of Nazeing where the Riggs family resided, had been a center of Puritan activity for decades. Successive bishops of London, however, let them practice their beliefs without any interference. But a new bishop appointed in 1628 required strict adherence to church law and made it impossible for them to stay in Essex County.[2] They realized their only chance at reforming the Church of England from within might be to model a "Godly" community in the New World.

In the first major wave of emigration after Pilgrims departed, a group led by Puritan lawyer John Winthrop set out in 1630 to establish Massachusetts Bay Colony. A fleet of 11 ships led by *Arbella,* along with six other ships that arrived a few months later, delivered from 700 to 1,000 colonists during summer 1630. Numbers increased during the next three years when followers of Puritan minister John Eliot, known as Nazeing Christians, arrived at the Massachusetts colony. Most of Eliot's contingent settled about three miles south of Boston at a town they named Roxbury. It included the Riggs family.

Edward, predecessor of Riggs branches that made their way to Boone County, Missouri, most likely was born in 1589. An unnamed son of a Richard Riggs is listed in baptism records for that year from St. Peter's Church in Roydon, Essex County, England. This town is less than five miles from Nazeing, where he married Elizabeth Holmes in 1618 at All Saints Church.[3] Elizabeth had been baptized in this church in 1590, and all five Riggs children followed this tradition. The family practiced their Puritan beliefs at All Saints, established in the 11th century. The church remains today as a Congregationalist denomination.

Immigration of Essex County ministers and laymen between 1631 and 1633 differed from 1620 Pilgrim arrivals at Plymouth Rock and Winthrop's Fleet landings in 1630.[4] These earlier migrations were organized top-down, with a few affluent laymen making all preparations. Leaders purchased or leased ships for their voyage, subsidized and loaded provisions, recruited passengers and made sure that at least one minister sailed with them. Soldiers and individuals having useful skills, such as builders, craftsmen, barrel makers and blacksmiths, became part of the crew.

That changed with Essex immigrants, and migration became more spontaneous. A charismatic Puritan minister, in this case John Eliot, or a wealthy Puritan layman gathered a few families and proceeded to the docks, where they joined similar groups. Families paid for passage and provisions, and the ship's crew did not worry about what skills passengers possessed. This bottom-up process attracted passengers more likely to include women and children. It paved the way for larger migration of families from England between 1634 and 1640.

The Riggs family, with their youngest child less than a year old, left Nazeing and arrived at Massachusetts Bay Colony in May 1633 after seven weeks at sea. Though passenger lists for individual ships did not exist, most likely they sailed on *Mary and Jane*, which carried 196 passengers. Only one other vessel arrived that month, but it carried just 30 passengers and at least ten cows.[5] Sailing on all ships at that time was an ordeal, often caused by rough seas launched by gale-force winds and violent storms. Food supplies had to be rationed, and illnesses and deaths took their toll. With such severe conditions, immigrants bound for Massachusetts Bay observed strict regulations, and swift punishment followed offenses. In a typical journal entry, Capt. John Winthrop wrote:

Map of Massachusetts drawn by William Wood in 1633, the year the Riggs family arrived (Published in his New Englands Prospect, *1635)*

We kept a fast aboard our ship . . . The wind continued still very high at [West] and [South] and rainy. In the time of our fast, two of our landmen pierced a rundlet [wine cask-sized barrel] of strong water, and stole some of it, for which we laid them in bolts all the night, and the next morning the principal was openly whipped, and both kept with bread and water that day.[6]

When the Riggses stepped onto American soil in 1633, wretched conditions continued. Along with other illnesses and diseases, a deadly smallpox epidemic raged throughout New England that year. Many colonists succumbed, but this plague had more widespread consequences among Native Americans in the region. Unlike English settlers, they had never been exposed to smallpox and had no immunity. Native populations in New England dropped by more than 70 percent, and some tribes lost up to 95 percent of their members.[7] Nature struck blows to colonists as well, including severe weather along the seacoast. During one winter, five men and a young girl attempted to travel from Massachusetts Bay to Plymouth by boat, despite warnings from more experienced seafarers. When the vessel filled with water, their legs became frozen into blocks of ice. Native Americans took these ill-

Old Roxbury Burying Grounds. Lydia Riggs, daughter of Edward and Elizabeth Riggs who died in 1633, is believed to be the first burial in this cemetery. Other Riggs family members are buried here as well. (Photograph by Tim Pierce)

fated travelers to their camp and tried to thaw them out. Despite best efforts to nurse them back to health, all five men died, though the young girl survived this ordeal.[8]

Riggs family members did not escape heartaches during their first years in the colony. Less than three months after arrival, daughter Lydia, age 10, died. Her August 1633 burial is believed to be the first interment at Old Roxbury Burying Grounds. The following year brought deaths of Edward's wife, Elizabeth, and two additional children, Elizabeth, 6, and John, 5.[9] It is unknown whether smallpox killed them or whether they contracted other illnesses rampant aboard ships and in the colony. Edward remarried in 1635, this time to Elizabeth Roosa, to provide a mother for his two surviving children, Edward II, 15, and Mary, 2.[10]

The Puritan church in Roxbury admitted Edward in 1633 and gave him full voting rights in 1634. This status enabled him to assist in governance and participate fully in church and community affairs. Upon entering this colony, settlers such as Edward became closely monitored to make sure they fit the church's ideal of a Godly man. After proving himself worthy, the church hierarchy accepted him and allowed Edward to take an oath of allegiance to the church. Puritan beliefs did not permit women to become members or vote.[11] Though Puritans enjoyed freedom of worship, they had no tolerance for opposing religious or political views. A General Court enforced strict laws that governed most aspects of life, including business dealings, social relations,

religious affairs and family matters. Along with swift retribution for capital crimes, these laws punished people for such things as kissing in public, using foul language, missing church, drinking to excess, laziness, gluttony, violating dress regulations, smoking in streets, courting a girl without her parents' permission, fighting, selling poorly made products, having a bad attitude, gossiping and more. Puritans meted out harsh punishments for committing such sins, believing God's wrath against violators would be far worse if left uncorrected.

Similar to what some Puritans suffered in England, discipline included dunking stools, fines, imprisonment, whipping, pillories or stocks, tar and feathering, banishment, ears cut off, burning, a hot awl through the tongue and public hanging. Examples of such sentences abound in early records. On one occasion a man returning from a three-year ocean voyage kissed his wife on their doorstep and spent two hours in the stocks for "lewd and unseemly behavior."[12] Another man had to stand in public with the word "Drunkard" written on his back and then wore a red "D" for a year after his second offense. Abel Buell, who later printed the first map of the United States, minted counterfeit money and had the tip of his ear cut off, along with being branded on his forehead.[13] Puritans believed God would protect them if they strictly obeyed religious rules. If they did not, colonists would be punished. In their dogma, God ordained everything that happened in their lives. For example, John Winthrop's journal of Aug. 6, 1633, tells of two men who drowned gathering oysters after their boat floated away when the

Puritan family at Massachusetts Bay Colony

tide came in. "It was an evident judgment of God upon them," he wrote, "for they were wicked persons." Another journal entry, on Feb. 26, 1633, tells the story of two little girls plucking feathers while sitting under a heap of logs. Their mother asked them to move, since wind was blowing feathers into their house. "They were no sooner gone, but the whole heap of logs fell down in the place, and [would have] crushed them to death, if the Lord, in his special providence, had not delivered them."[14]

The church, as arbiter of religious and social life, occupied the center of each town. Law required that all houses be built within half a mile of the religious meeting house for mutual protection.[15] Education had great significance in the colony. Puritans believed that faithful people could commune directly with God by reading the Bible. Therefore, learning to read became a high priority. In 1642, Massachusetts passed the first laws governing education in America. A compulsory attendance law did not require children to go to school, but it stated that all Massachusetts heads of household were responsible for "education" of any children living under their roof (including children of servants and apprentices).[16] Importance of education passed down through successive Riggs family generations.

John Eliot, who led Nazeing Christians to this New World, taught in Roxbury's church for 60 years and served as its sole preacher for 40 years. He also earned the title "Apostle to the Indians" for his work educating and ministering to Native Americans. Colonists had trade agreements and friendly relations with many tribes, but encounters were not always cordial. Efforts to control fur trade and other tensions led to an armed conflict between 1636 and 1638. It involved the Pequot tribe against colonists in Massachusetts and Connecticut and their Native American allies.

During this war, John Winthrop cited Riggs for bravery in what became known as the Great Swamp Fight in July 1637. Pequots fled to the far side of a swamp near present-day Fairfield, Connecticut. The commander of colonial troops ordered his company to go around the swamp, but some members did not hear his order. Instead, they faced attacking dogs, flying arrows and danger from being swallowed into the bog. Edward and others fought off Indians to rescue trapped men, some gravely wounded. In a July 28, 1637, letter to William Bradford, Governor of Plymouth Colony, Winthrop wrote that the men "were in great danger to have been taken by the Indians, but Sergeant Rigges [sic], and Jeffery and two or three more rescued them, and slew diverse of the Indians with their swords."[17] Puritan clergyman William Hubbard, in his narrative of the colony's early years, wrote about some who made it out of the swamp, "They were rescued at great peril by Serjeant [sic] Riggs of Roxbury."[18]

Roxbury housed many wealthy colonists, including prominent people from Boston and nine early colonial governors. Edward and his family owned land but lived a simple existence. In a 1652 Roxbury land inventory, he possessed seven parcels: his house and barn on

"First Landing Party of the Founders of Newark," by Gutzon Borglum honors Puritans who established the city in 1666. Names inscribed on the back include Edward Riggs II and his adult son Joseph.

five acres; three acres on an end of "Great Lots;" seven acres on the highway; one acre of meadowland; a salt marsh; 13 acres in Nookes division, and ten acres near Dedham.[19] These acquisitions included land grants provided to original colonists. Edward died in 1670, a year after his second wife. Probate records indicate a spartan household, consisting of a feather bed and bed linens, table settings, kitchen equipment, men's clothing, a chest, and a cupboard. His inventory value totaled 128 pounds 7 shillings. Of this amount, 93 pounds were in real estate, including land sold just before his death.[20]

By the time Edward died, immigration to Massachusetts Bay Colony had dwindled from its former highs. In 1633 the Bishop of London had been elevated to Archbishop of Canterbury, meaning he could persecute Puritans throughout England, rather than just Essex County. This had led to dramatic increases in immigration throughout the remainder of this decade. Beginning in 1640, however, immigration slowed due largely to additional jobs being created in England, as well as reinstating Parliament. Puritans began to believe once again that they might achieve their religious goals without having to leave the country. Thus, the period between 1620 (*The Mayflower* sailing) and 1640 became known as The Great Migration. During those 20 years about 20,000 English men, women and children crossed the Atlantic to America.[21]

Declining immigration and aging original colonists caused Puritans to become concerned about spiritual disinterest. In 1679, leaders blamed an increase in moral violations and made laws even stricter, driving away more colonists. Eventually, Puritans relaxed their church membership standards, and religious fervor diminished. The word "Puritan" disappeared, and members became known primarily as Congregationalists. Edward Riggs II, surviving son of Edward Riggs I, displayed his concern about moral decay. By 1640 he had married yet another Elizabeth and moved with his family to Milford, Connecticut, part of New Haven Colony. It held more strictly to old Puritan virtues than nearby colonies. About 15 years later Edward II's family and a few other colonists moved about ten miles north up the

Naugatuck River to establish another Puritan settlement at Derby, Connecticut. Family land there still is referred to as "Riggs Hill."

Still not satisfied with earlier attempts to establish a perfect theocracy (government by divine guidance, Edward II and some neighbors had an opportunity to acquire land in the English Province of the Jerseys. In 1666 a group of 11 men scouted out a suitable location. After finding an ideal spot, about half of their group, including Edward II, remained to complete arrangements. Others returned to Connecticut to prepare for their move. Edward II's family chose to join him immediately, becoming the first family to live in the settlement that became Newark, New Jersey.[22] When matters related to this relocation required Edward II to return temporarily to Milford, his wife remained in New Jersey under difficult circumstances. As a reward for her many sacrifices during this time, Newark leaders gave Elizabeth additional acreage added to their home lot.[23]

Riggs family branches ventured westward during successive generations. The branch ultimately settling in Missouri went first to Morristown, New Jersey; then to Surry County, North Carolina, and on to Lincoln County, Kentucky, before permanently locating in Boone County, Missouri. Zadok Riggs, third great grandson of his immigrant ancestor Edward Riggs, left his large horse farm in Kentucky and arrived with his family in Boone County during 1816 to take advantage of available government land grants. He first settled in the Perche Creek area near Columbia, but after eight years moved to land about 12 miles north of Columbia to avoid

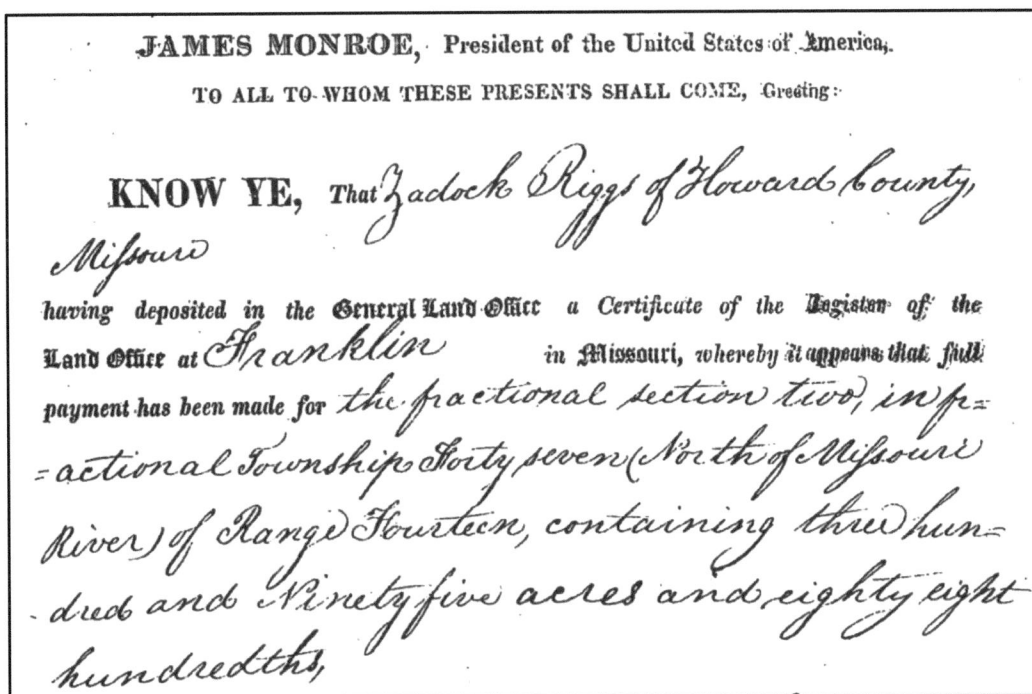

JAMES MONROE, President of the United States of America,

TO ALL TO WHOM THESE PRESENTS SHALL COME, Greeting:

KNOW YE, That *Zadock Riggs of Howard County, Missouri* having deposited in the General Land Office a Certificate of the Register of the Land Office at *Franklin* in Missouri, whereby it appears that full payment has been made for *the fractional section two, in fractional Township Forty seven (North of Missouri River) of Range Fourteen, containing three hundred and Ninety five acres and eighty eight hundredths,*

Excerpt from the first of several federal land grants issued to Zadok Riggs for public lands in Howard County area that became Boone County. This patent was issued Sept. 11, 1820.

Lithograph print of University of Missouri Campus, ca. 1850. From left, President's House, Academic Building and Observatory. (University Archives)

malarial conditions.[24] The family encountered other problems in the bottomlands. One of Zadok's sons, Samuel, suffered a rabid wolf bite while sleeping in a cave near the creek. He immediately returned to Kentucky for a madstone (a rock-like substance of calcium deposits and other materials formed in the stomach of a deer), which the family insisted provided a successful cure. Pioneers believed it had medicinal properties that could draw out poison from an animal bite.

After the family moved to the new community of Rocky Fork, Zadok built a schoolhouse with help from his neighbors. Like his Puritan ancestors and generations to come, Zadok believed education important to success in life, and the Riggs family participated in establishing the University of Missouri in Columbia. Boone County and Columbia residents pledged $117,921 (an astonishing $3.9 million in today's dollars) in cash and land during 1839 to outbid five other counties vying for location of the state's land grant university.[25] "Old Zadok," as people called Riggs, occupied

community and political positions that made him well-known and respected. He had become a major landowner and businessman, including blacksmith, grist mill operator and mechanic. For many years the *Statesman* newspaper offices in Columbia displayed his "Old Continental" Revolutionary War waistcoat made in Virginia by his wife in 1775. Zadok owned slaves, but he freed them in 1846, about 20 years before the Emancipation Proclamation.[26]

When his great granddaughter Nancy "Nannie" Riggs wed George Foster Snoddy from adjacent Howard County in 1878, their marriage united two of the region's earliest and most prominent families. Like the Riggs family, Snoddys landed in this country well before the American Revolution and made their way to Missouri with other patriots after the War of 1812. The Riggs name carried through succeeding generations and serves as a reminder of their bravery and sacrifices to aid in creation of the new nation.

Riggs Direct Line: East Coast Branch

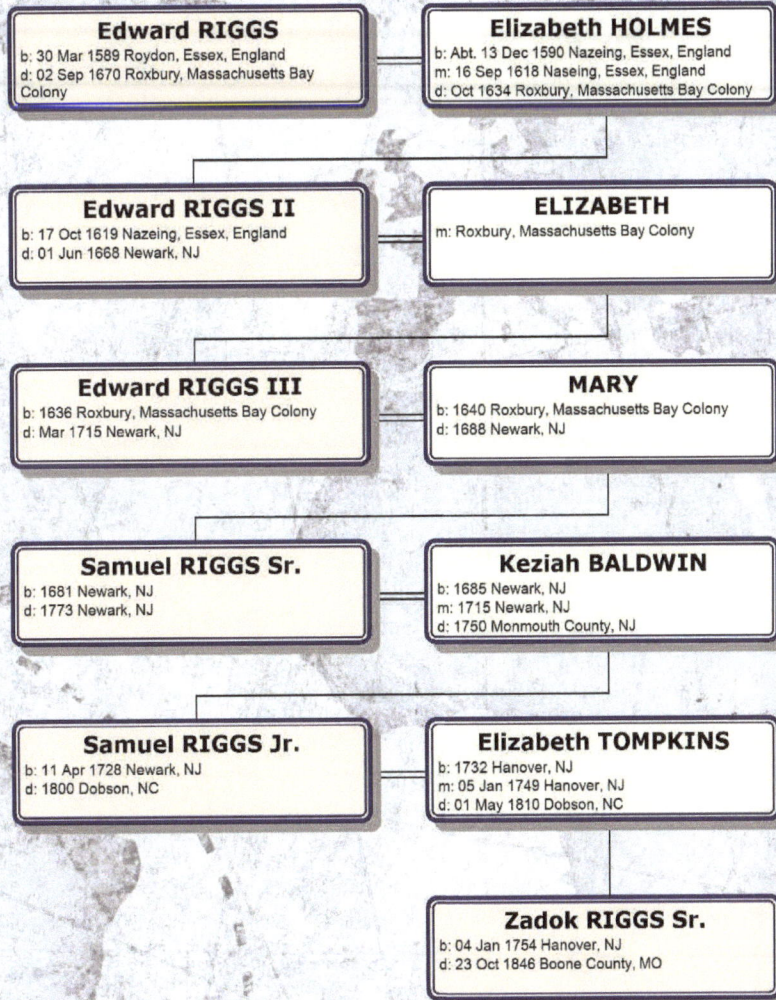

Edward RIGGS
b: 30 Mar 1589 Roydon, Essex, England
d: 02 Sep 1670 Roxbury, Massachusetts Bay Colony

Elizabeth HOLMES
b: Abt. 13 Dec 1590 Nazeing, Essex, England
m: 16 Sep 1618 Naseing, Essex, England
d: Oct 1634 Roxbury, Massachusetts Bay Colony

Edward RIGGS II
b: 17 Oct 1619 Nazeing, Essex, England
d: 01 Jun 1668 Newark, NJ

ELIZABETH
m: Roxbury, Massachusetts Bay Colony

Edward RIGGS III
b: 1636 Roxbury, Massachusetts Bay Colony
d: Mar 1715 Newark, NJ

MARY
b: 1640 Roxbury, Massachusetts Bay Colony
d: 1688 Newark, NJ

Samuel RIGGS Sr.
b: 1681 Newark, NJ
d: 1773 Newark, NJ

Keziah BALDWIN
b: 1685 Newark, NJ
m: 1715 Newark, NJ
d: 1750 Monmouth County, NJ

Samuel RIGGS Jr.
b: 11 Apr 1728 Newark, NJ
d: 1800 Dobson, NC

Elizabeth TOMPKINS
b: 1732 Hanover, NJ
m: 05 Jan 1749 Hanover, NJ
d: 01 May 1810 Dobson, NC

Zadok RIGGS Sr.
b: 04 Jan 1754 Hanover, NJ
d: 23 Oct 1846 Boone County, MO

Riggs Direct Line: Missouri Branch

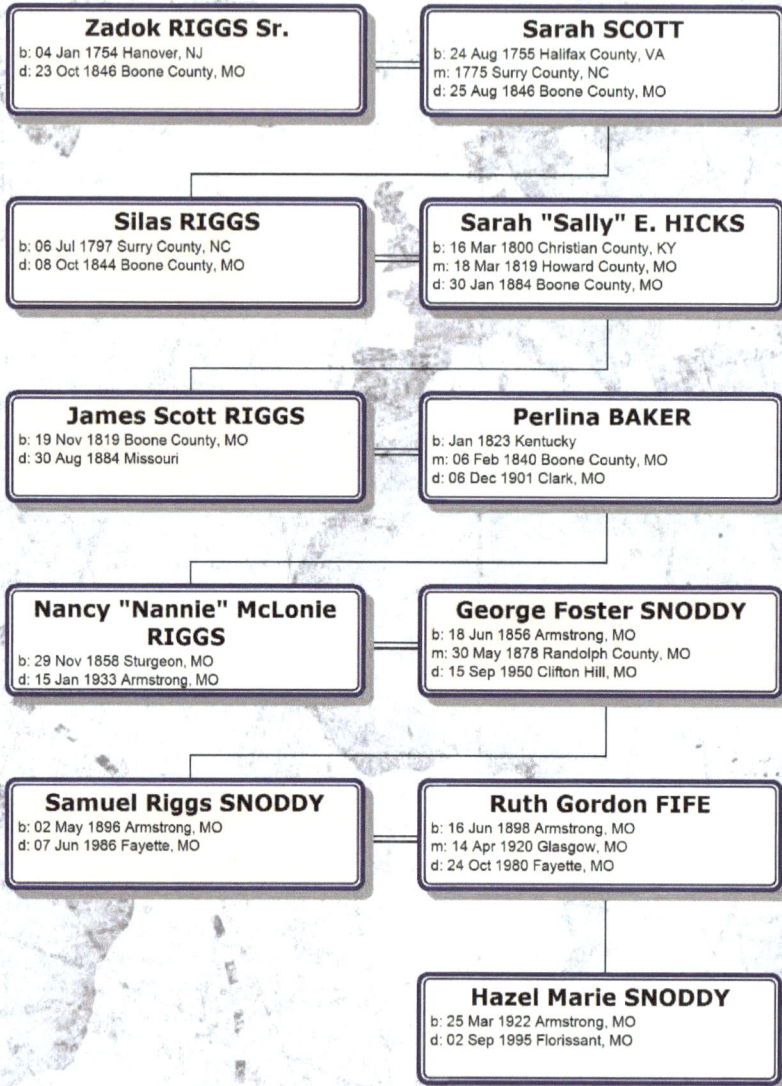

Zadok RIGGS Sr.
b: 04 Jan 1754 Hanover, NJ
d: 23 Oct 1846 Boone County, MO

Sarah SCOTT
b: 24 Aug 1755 Halifax County, VA
m: 1775 Surry County, NC
d: 25 Aug 1846 Boone County, MO

Silas RIGGS
b: 06 Jul 1797 Surry County, NC
d: 08 Oct 1844 Boone County, MO

Sarah "Sally" E. HICKS
b: 16 Mar 1800 Christian County, KY
m: 18 Mar 1819 Howard County, MO
d: 30 Jan 1884 Boone County, MO

James Scott RIGGS
b: 19 Nov 1819 Boone County, MO
d: 30 Aug 1884 Missouri

Perlina BAKER
b: Jan 1823 Kentucky
m: 06 Feb 1840 Boone County, MO
d: 06 Dec 1901 Clark, MO

Nancy "Nannie" McLonie RIGGS
b: 29 Nov 1858 Sturgeon, MO
d: 15 Jan 1933 Armstrong, MO

George Foster SNODDY
b: 18 Jun 1856 Armstrong, MO
m: 30 May 1878 Randolph County, MO
d: 15 Sep 1950 Clifton Hill, MO

Samuel Riggs SNODDY
b: 02 May 1896 Armstrong, MO
d: 07 Jun 1986 Fayette, MO

Ruth Gordon FIFE
b: 16 Jun 1898 Armstrong, MO
m: 14 Apr 1920 Glasgow, MO
d: 24 Oct 1980 Fayette, MO

Hazel Marie SNODDY
b: 25 Mar 1922 Armstrong, MO
d: 02 Sep 1995 Florissant, MO

End Notes

1 Samuel Rawson Gardiner, *History of England from the Accession of James I to the Outbreak of the Civil War, 1603-1642,* vol. 8 (London: Longmans, Green, and Co., 1909) 150, 224-249.

2 Robert Charles Anderson, "The Importance of Essex to the Great Migration to New England in the Early 1630s," *Historian,* Essex Society for Family History. Reprinted in *Nazeing History,* Spring 2021 (nazeinghistory.org).

3 Marriage of Edward Riggs and Elizabeth Holmes, Essex Records Office, All Saints Church, "Parish Marriage Records 1559-1669" (essexarchivesonline.co.uk).

4 Anderson, "The Importance of Essex to the Great Migration."

5 Meredith B. Colket, Jr., *Founders of Early American Families: Emigrants from Europe, 1607-1657.* (Cleveland: General Court of the Order of Founders and Patriots of America, 1975), 243 (Ancestry.com); John Winthrop Journal, *"History of New England, 1630-1649"* (New York, Barnes & Noble, 1959), 100.

6 Winthrop's Journal, 25.

7 "The Impact of European Diseases," *Mashantucket Pequot Museum and Research Center,* Mashantucket, CT (pequotmuseum.org).

8 Winthrop's Journal, 55-56.

9 Roxbury Deaths, "Massachusetts, U.S., Town and Vital Records, 1620-1988," vol. 1 (Ancestry.com).

10 "Vital Records of Roxbury, Massachusetts, to the End of the Year 1849," vol. 2 (Essex Institute: Salem, Mass., 1926), 346 (Ancestry.com).

11 H. F. Andrews, *List of freemen, Massachusetts Bay colony from 1630 to 1691* (Exira, IA: Exira Printing Co., 1906), 32 (archive.org).

12 Kathy Alexander, "Puritans of New England," *Legends of America,* updated January 2023 (legendsofamerica.com/puritans).

13 "Way More than the Scarlet Letter: Puritan Punishments," *New England Historical Society* (newenglandhistoricalsociety.com).

14 Winthrop's Journal, 99, 103.

15 Charles M. Ellis, *The History of Roxbury Town* (Boston: Samuel G. Drake, 1847), 139.

16 Dave Roos, "What School Was Like in the 13 Colonies," *History,* 8 Jun 2023 (history.com/news).

17 *Winthrop Papers 1498-1654,* cited in Robert Charles Anderson, *The Great Migration Begins: Immigrants to New England, 1620-1633,* vol. 3 (Boston: New England Historic and Genealogical Society, 1995), 1585 (Ancestry.com).

18 Samuel G. Drake, *The History and Antiquities of Boston* (Boston: Luther Stevens, 1856) 216. (Google.com/books).

19 "Roxbury Land and Church Records," *A Report of the Record Commissioners* [76] 55 (Boston: Rockwell and Churchhill, 1881), 37.

20 "Suffolk County (Massachusetts) Probate Records, 1636-1899," vol. 5-7, 1666-1674; (Ancestry.com).

21 Anderson, "The Importance of Essex to the Great Migration."

22 Wallace, John Hankins, "Genealogy of the Riggs Family," 1902 (FamilySearch.org).

23 Robert Charles Anderson and Alvy Ray Smith, "The Genealogy of Edward Riggs of Roxbury, Massachusetts, Revisited." *The Genealogist 23* (2009), 140.

24 Walter Williams, ed., "Turner Riggs biographical sketch," *History of Northeast Missouri,* vol. 3, (Chicago/New York: Lewis Publishing Co., 1913), 865.

25 William F. Switzer, *History of Boone County, Missouri* (St. Louis, Western Historical Co., 1882), 252-258.

26 Probate Records, Boone County, vol. A-B, 1821-1850; Missouri, County, District and Probate Courts, 792-795, (Ancestry.com).

"Boone's First View of Kentucky" by William Tylee Ranney, 1849. John Snoddy was among Daniel Boone's crew who cut the Wilderness Road into Kentucky in 1775. (Original painting a gift of the Thomas Gilcrease Foundation, Gilcrease Museum)

American Revolutionary War Spy
John Snoddy

When the American Revolutionary War comes to mind, one might think of George Washington crossing the Delaware, rather than an organized spy network. But Capt. John Snoddy, earliest known ancestor of the Snoddy branch that settled in Missouri, led one such important group. Based at Moore's Fort, also known as Snoddy's Fort, along Clinch River in Southwest Virginia, Snoddy's men served as "Indian Spies" looking for Native Americans allied with the British.

Moore's Fort, one of seven forts built along the Clinch River, provided protection on Virginia's western frontier. The colony's governor, John Murray, 4th Earl of Dunmore, ordered these forts to be built after hostilities escalated between settlers and mostly Shawnees, leading to Lord Dunmore's War in fall 1774. This brief campaign ended with a treaty in which Shawnees agreed to give up hunting grounds south of the Ohio River, opening a way for settlers to push westward into Kentucky. Despite this treaty, attacks continued on both sides for the next 20 years; peace existed only on paper.

Four of the seven forts, commanded by Capt. William Russell, protected settlements on the lower Clinch River. Named in honor of high-ranking military officers, none of the forts' official names stuck because they paid tribute to officers unknown to frontier settlers. Instead, settlers and soldiers referred to them by who owned the land or commanded the fort. Fort Byrd, located in Lower Castle's Woods, became Moore's Fort, referring to two brothers who owned the land, William and Joseph Moore. Largest of the forts on Clinch River, it housed about 20 families, along with a garrison of 20 to 25 men who patrolled the area.

In 1769, 30-year-old John Snoddy and others arrived at Castle's Woods in Southwest Virginia to form its first permanent settlement. Upon arrival, these men built a primitive palisade, including a two-story blockhouse with small gun ports instead of windows. They referred to it as Snoddy's Station. To warn of danger, lookouts fired guns or rang the fort's bell. Its inhabitants lived a primitive existence; meals typically consisted of hog, hominy and cornbread. Milk and mush sufficed for evening fare, sometimes accompanied by sweetened water, molasses, bear oil, or gravy. Venison and beef occasionally made it to the table; chicken was a delicacy usually reserved for company.[1] A few years after John arrived, his future father-in-law, John Walker Jr., came with his family from Augusta County, Virginia. They lived in Lower Castle's Woods, where Walker owned a 300-acre farm known as Broad Meadows on Sinking Creek. Walker

Castle's Woods is named for Jacob Castle, a hunter who traded a musket and a butcher knife to Native Americans for a small tract on the Clinch River. He is believed to have had a Shawnee wife. (Artwork is from a book on Castle, written by Linda Banton-Trush Sandow)

and his wife, Ann Houston Walker, had eight children, including six daughters who intermarried with other original families.[2] Their daughter Margaret Houston Walker married Snoddy in 1774, and they moved into the recently completed and more secure Moore's Fort for protection.

Daniel Boone and his family also resided at Moore's Fort. They arrived at Castle's Woods in late 1773 after Boone's son, James, and others died by Native American hands during Boone's first attempt to establish a Kentucky settlement. Thwarted settlers fell back to Snoddy's Station, from where members of Boone's party returned to their homes. Having sold their house and furnishings in North Carolina prior to setting out for Kentucky, Boone's family had no residence and accepted an invitation to stay the winter at Snoddy's Station. Winter stretched into almost two years, however, after Boone accepted command of Moore's Fort, completed not long after his arrival. He also had responsibility for Russell's Fort, four miles north at Upper Castle's Woods, and Blackmore's Fort, 16 miles below. While at Moore's Fort, Rebecca Boone bore another son, William, who died shortly after his birth and is buried in an unmarked grave in the old Moore's Fort cemetery.

A resident of Moore's Fort at that time, Mrs. Samuel Scott, describes in her memoirs an amusing incident in the fort while the Boones were there. Fed up with men being lax in their guard duties and spending too much time outside the fort playing ball and other activities,

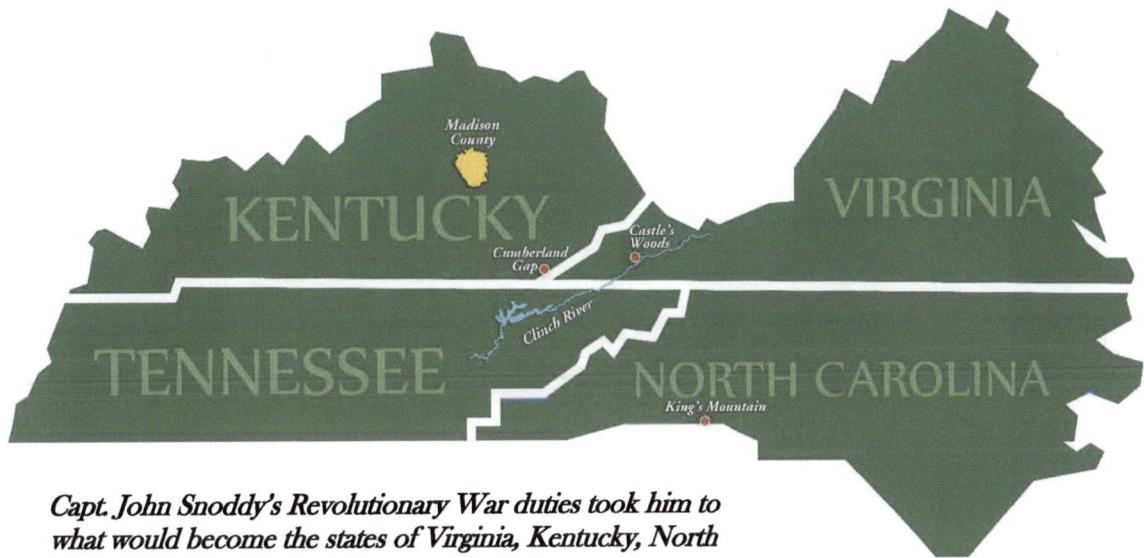

Capt. John Snoddy's Revolutionary War duties took him to what would become the states of Virginia, Kentucky, North Carolina and Tennessee.

Mrs. Boone and other women loaded their guns, sneaked outside the fort, and closed the gates behind them. When they began firing in the air, men thought they were being attacked and scrambled toward the fort. Some took a short cut through a pond in their haste. Unable to get back into the fort, one man climbed over the fence and opened a gate. After the prank, some frantic men wanted these women whipped, but most likely the women got their point across without punishment.[3]

Though settlers felt safe inside forts, few protections existed for those outside, including Native Americans. In one heinous act, frontiersmen slaughtered relatives of a Mingo leader known by his American name, John Logan. Though details vary, victims included Logan's brother, his pregnant sister and other kin, murdered while they socialized with white settlers at a house near the mouth of Yellow Creek. Logan had long been a friend to

Virginia settlers, but this brutal attack transformed him into a bitter enemy. His vendetta became a precursor to the brief Lord Dunmore's War, in which Virginia Colonials won a victory against several Native nations.

Logan refused to attend a peace treaty signing, but he sent a letter instead. Later, Thomas Jefferson published this letter, which became known as Logan's Lament, in his *Notes on the State of Virginia.* The letter states in part: "There runs not a drop of my blood in the veins of any living creature. This has called on me for revenge. I have sought it: I have killed many: I have fully glutted my vengeance. . . . Who is there to mourn for Logan? Not one."[4]

With land south of the Ohio River now belonging to Virginia, adventurous pioneers began pushing into this newly opened territory. In 1775 a private North Carolina

Capt. John Snoddy assisted in building Fort Boonesborough. Boone's journal noted that "The chimneys, with huge open fire places, were built outside of the cabins, but inside the stockade. . . . The windows and doors of the cabins were within the stockade. The heavy wooden gates were closed with bars of stout wood. . . . When danger threatened, the cattle and horses were kept in the open space in the middle. Every cow and every horse wore a bell. (Postcard depiction of the fort)

company hired Daniel Boone to cut a road through wilderness via Cumberland Gap and establish a fort in Kentucky. Capt. Snoddy served with approximately 30 men who accompanied Boone on this second trip into Kentucky, hacking their way through nearly 300 miles of territory to establish Wilderness Road. This trail became a route west for about 300,000 settlers during the next 35 years. It led to Kentucky's first permanent settlement at Boonesborough, as well as Kentucky's admission to the Union as the 15th state in 1792.[5]

In a court deposition recording Kentucky's early history, Snoddy said, "I came to Kentucky with Daniel Boone in the year 1775 and came by the blue lick crost [sic] Silver Creek and went up Harts Fork and soon on to what is now Bonnesbourgh [sic]."[6] After three weeks through rough terrain, Boone selected a site on Kentucky River's south bank to build a fortification, named Fort Boonesborough in recognition of his leadership.

Upon completion of this fort, which took 2 ½ months, many frontiersmen, including Boone and the Moore brothers, returned to Moore's Fort long enough to collect their families and return to Boonesborough. Snoddy, however, purchased Moore's Fort from the departing Moores and remained there with his family. He also accepted a commission as militia captain, with this fortified settlement once again being referred to as Snoddy's Fort.[7] By then the Revolutionary War had begun, and hostilities on Virginia's frontier increased. Though some Native Americans sided with Patriots, British officers recruited many Native nations to their cause, supplying them with arms and often instigating attacks. A company of spies, led by Captain Snoddy, attempted to thwart this activity. They normally did not engage with the enemy, but rather forayed deep into ominous wilderness, searching Indian trails for evidence of approaching Native Americans or suspicious activity. Attacks heightened between April and September when weather remained pleasant and foliage provided cover. Additionally, settlers were more likely to be working in their fields with no protection. Sometimes balmy weather lasted into October and November, supposedly giving rise to the term "Indian Summer." Violent collisions between patriots and British, along with Indian allies on both sides, often led to sadistic brutality by all.

With war underway, Virginia males 16 to 50 were considered militia "volunteers" in their counties.[8] Recruits chosen to be spies were divided into groups of two and four, with each group assigned a frontier section, covering about 150 miles of rugged wilderness. Volunteers signed up for three- to nine-month tours, which sometimes meant being away from their fort and families for weeks at a time,

returning periodically for supplies or to report suspicious activity. Spies carried supplies on their backs and foraged for food. They slept on the ground and could not build a fire for fear of being spotted. Private Alexander Ritchie Jr.'s description of his spy service under Snoddy in his pension application probably is typical. He and his partner left the fort on Monday mornings, packed their provisions on their backs, and ranged through mountains for a week before returning to the fort on Sundays.[9]

British officers countered with Loyalist spies, also referred to as Tories or King's Men. They came from colonists who remained loyal to the British Crown during this revolution. Sorting Patriots from Loyalists proved difficult, as they might even be next-door neighbors hiding their sentiments, making it hard for both sides to know who to trust.

Patriot militia returning home after defeating Loyalists at King's Mountain. (From a print by Don Troiani)

Though the Revolutionary War officially ended in 1783, ferocious fighting with Native Americans on the western frontier continued. Capt. Snoddy served as commander at Crab Orchard Fort near Boonesborough at least until 1786 and dealt with occasional Indian raids. This painting by Andrew Knez Jr., titled "First Attack on Boonesborough," depicts a typical skirmish between settlers and Native Americans. (andrewknezjr.com)

On one occasion, Capt. William Campbell, commander of militias in Washington County, Kentucky, encountered an old man walking along the road with a bag of sticks over his shoulder. Campbell and his companions rode past him on their horses but grew suspicious when the man darted into the woods. After circling back and catching up they searched him, believing he might be a Tory spy. At first they found nothing. Then noticing that his shoes seemed new, they cut into the heels and found a letter from British military officials addressed to "The King of the Cherokees," with instructions for a coordinated attack. The man gave a full confession, but Campbell, who gained notoriety for his brutal treatment of Loyalists, hanged him.[10]

Sometimes Capt. Snoddy's duties went beyond overseeing spies. During summer 1778, Shawnees made a minor foray into Washington County, and Campbell sent Snoddy in pursuit. On June 3 Snoddy reported that he and two other officers chased their enemies as far as Rye Cove, southwest of Moore's Fort, but then lost them. As ordered, Snoddy also sent a man under guard accused of providing aid to a deserter. Despite this order, Snoddy pointed out that he knew the man to be a "well-wisher to the Cause," and the deserter he supposedly aided had been cleared of any wrong-doing.[11] Campbell may have released him, but given his reputation, that is unclear. Snoddy led another pursuit when Native Americans captured two girls and headed to Canada to sell them. He and men from Moore's Fort chased them, overtaking these kidnappers at what is now Floyd County,

Kentucky. In a running battle, one girl was tomahawked but survived, and the other escaped to safety among rescuers. Both were taken back to the fort, along with a wounded militiaman who would not survive his bullet wound.[12]

During spring and summer 1778, Native Americans stepped up British-supported attacks. Snoddy's sister-in-law, Ann Walker Cowan, barely survived capture by a Delaware war party in May 1778. Ann resided at Cowan's Fort in Upper Castle's Woods, four miles above Moore's Fort where her sister, Margaret Walker Snoddy, resided. Ann's husband, Samuel Cowan, had been killed in an attack outside the fort a year earlier. While Ann traveled between Cowan's Fort and Moore's Fort, a Cherokee raiding party captured and carried her off. On the same day, a different raiding party from the same group took her nephew William Walker, 8, while he plowed corn with another uncle, Samuel Walker. After killing Samuel and kidnapping William, both Cherokee groups met in nearby woods and headed toward Ohio with their captives. Later William said he and his aunt kept looking backward, hoping for a rescue party, but none came. Once they crossed the Ohio River, Cherokees sold Ann to a Northern Ohio tribe. She remained in captivity for seven years before being ransomed and allowed to return home. William went directly to a Delaware tribe settlement on Whetstone River, where a Native American family adopted him.[13]

Tragedies continued to befall the Snoddy family. Margaret Snoddy's first cousin, Capt. James Moore, moved his large family to a remote valley, miles from the nearest fort. He was killed while working in his field, along with two of his children who were carrying water from a stream. His wife and five additional children were taken, with three dead before arriving at a Shawnee village. His wife and oldest daughter were tortured and burned at the stake, and the remaining daughter sold to an unfriendly American. Two years prior to their deaths, the Moores' oldest son, James, had been captured. He lived with a Native American family for five years before being purchased by a French trader. Shortly before gaining his freedom, James learned about the deaths of his family members and whereabouts of his sister who had continuously suffered abuse at the hands of her brutish owner. James rescued her, and the two returned to what remained of their home.[14]

In 1780, Snoddy and his militia company left Moore's Fort to assume similar duties at Crab Orchard Fort near Boonesborough, Kentucky, including scouting along the Kentucky, Cumberland, Dix and Rockcastle rivers. Snoddy hadn't been there long when he and his company answered a call to travel East and join Patriot militias in a surprise attack at King's Mountain. This battle on October 7, fought on the South Carolina-North Carolina line, has been described by some historians as "the war's largest all-American fight."[15] Hearing that about 1,000 Loyalists had encamped atop King's Mountain and threatened North Carolina's western frontier, an almost equal number of Patriots, later referred to as "over-mountain men," joined together to drive them out. These frontiersmen, familiar with King's Mountain's rugged terrain, charged directly up the steep mountain from all sides and began firing on their exposed enemies. Loyalist troops surrendered, delaying the British advance into North Carolina.[16]

Capt. Snoddy received a land grant for his service, consisting of 1,000 acres in Lincoln County, Kentucky, near Crab Orchard. The Washington County 1781 court record reads: "John Snoddy producing sufficient proof to the court that he was possessed of a preemption [land grant] for one thousand acres of land in the county of Kentucky; that he sent the same along with Daniel Boon [sic] and it was lost and that he never received a warrant for the same."[17] A land survey places his holdings between Drowning Creek and Dreaming Creek, just outside of Boonesborough, where Snoddy had initially come with Daniel Boone in 1775. Given his new land in Kentucky, Snoddy sold Moore's Fort and moved his wife and children to Kentucky.

Snoddy remained in command at Crab Orchard Fort at least until 1786, according to a deposition from one of his men, Oswald Townsen. Townsen states that Snoddy led about 100 soldiers on a march to turn them over to Col. Benjamin Logan for a campaign against Shawnees.[18] That same year, Snoddy received a commission from Governor Patrick Henry qualifying him as Colonel of Militia. Henry, one of America's founding fathers, served twice as Virginia's governor, but is best

Col. John Snoddy and his wife, Margaret, are buried at the Richmond Cemetery in Madison County, Kentucky. His grave bears a Revolutionary War commemorative marker. (Find a Grave, Old Joseph)

remembered for his pre-Revolutionary declaration, "Give me liberty, or give me death!" Henry also appointed Snoddy as a Commissioner of the Peace in Kentucky, then still part of Virginia. As such, Snoddy presided at the organization of Madison County, carved out of Lincoln County. He served in numerous capacities in the new county, including Justice of the Peace, Justice of the Quarter Sessions of the Court of Madison County, Commissioner of Revenue for Taxation, and first high sheriff of the county.[19]

Snoddy and his wife Margaret remained permanently in Madison County where they raised ten children. Over the years, he acquired additional acreage, but his heirs sold some of it after his death in 1814. Transactions totaling 135 acres on Silver Creek were just a fraction of the large tracts of land Snoddy owned in the county along various waterways.[20] Snoddy's wife, Margaret, lived another 17 years after his death, and they are buried in the Richmond Cemetery of Madison County. Along with a tombstone, his gravesite contains a plaque commemorating his distinguished Revolutionary War Service.

The Snoddy cemetery in Armstrong, Missouri, includes 17 marked graves and at least a dozen more. Joseph Walker Snoddy's stone is in the foreground. Grave of his son Samuel Walker Snoddy, father of George Foster Snoddy, is the broken stone at back right.

Mounted Volunteer Militia and became a standard bearer in the army of Gen. William Henry Harrison.[21] Known as "Old Tippecanoe," Harrison destroyed Native American confederacy headquarters near the Tippecanoe River in Indiana. He served as U.S. President for one month before dying in office. After the War of 1812, government warrants* led Joseph from Kentucky to Howard County, Missouri, where he received 480 acres in land grants for his service.[22] Two other siblings joined him in this 1813 move, along with a number of other Madison County residents seeking a new frontier. George Singleton Foster and his wife, Hannah Kerr, joined them, and six years after the move, their daughter, Narcissa, married Joseph. They had at least ten known children, but their second child, Foster, did not survive until his first birthday. He is buried on their farm in a spot that became the Snoddy family cemetery.

When her husband died in 1853, Narcissa raised their younger children.[23] For Narcissa, hardship and heartache haunted her family, including personal loss and splintered family relationships. Their children were born between 1820 and 1845, making her five living sons a prime age for service in the Civil War. Missouri became a divided state, and the Snoddy boys chose to fight for the Confederacy. Two of them died; one at the Battle of Pea Ridge in Arkansas and the other at an unverified location. Prior to the war, two

Colonel Snoddy wasn't the only family member to go to war during these early years. One of his sons, Joseph Walker Snoddy, served in the War of 1812 with the Kentucky

---

* *Land given by the federal government to non-commissioned officers and soldiers who served in the War of 1812.*

of Narcissa's daughters married Denny brothers, also from a pioneering Howard County family, and the Dennys fought for the Union. One brother, Capt. Alexander Denny of the Missouri Militia, led raids in the area, including ransacking the Snoddy farm that belonged to his mother-in-law. Union raiders stole horses, livestock and fodder, and burned barns and outbuildings in attempts to cut off food supply and horses that sustained Confederate bushwhackers in their lawless attacks against Federals.[24] This guerilla activity became especially intense in the "Little Dixie" area* home to legendary outlaws Frank and Jesse James. During the war, the James brothers joined "Bloody Bill" Anderson's gang in perpetrating some of the most vicious acts against Union troops and pro-Union citizens.[25] The intense fighting on both sides cut deeply into the Snoddy and Denny families and left lasting scars. For years after the Civil War, resentment festered on both sides, particularly since the Dennys fared much better financially than the Snoddys at war's end.

In later years, Joseph and Narcissa Snoddys' grandson, George Foster Snoddy, became one of Howard County's most prominent businessmen. Married to Nannie Riggs of neighboring Boone County, he ran a lumber company with various partners, including his brother Jeff Snoddy. A charter member of the Baptist church in Armstrong and a deacon for 70 years, he died at age 94.[26] George and Nannie experienced loss when a daughter,

Bertha, died before her first birthday, and a second daughter, Hazel Marie, died of shock after an appendectomy at age 18.[27] Her closest brother, Samuel Riggs (Sam) Snoddy, later named his own daughter after his younger sister. By the time Sam Snoddy married Ruth Gordon Fife, whose mother was a Denny, the Snoddy-Denny bad blood had become a thing of the past.

George Foster Snoddy and Nannie Riggs Snoddy at their home in Armstrong, MO, ca. 1930.

---

* *Little Dixie refers to a 13-county area along the Missouri River with similarities to states in the upper and lower South, particularly in their slave-based production of hemp and tobacco.*

Snoddy Direct Line

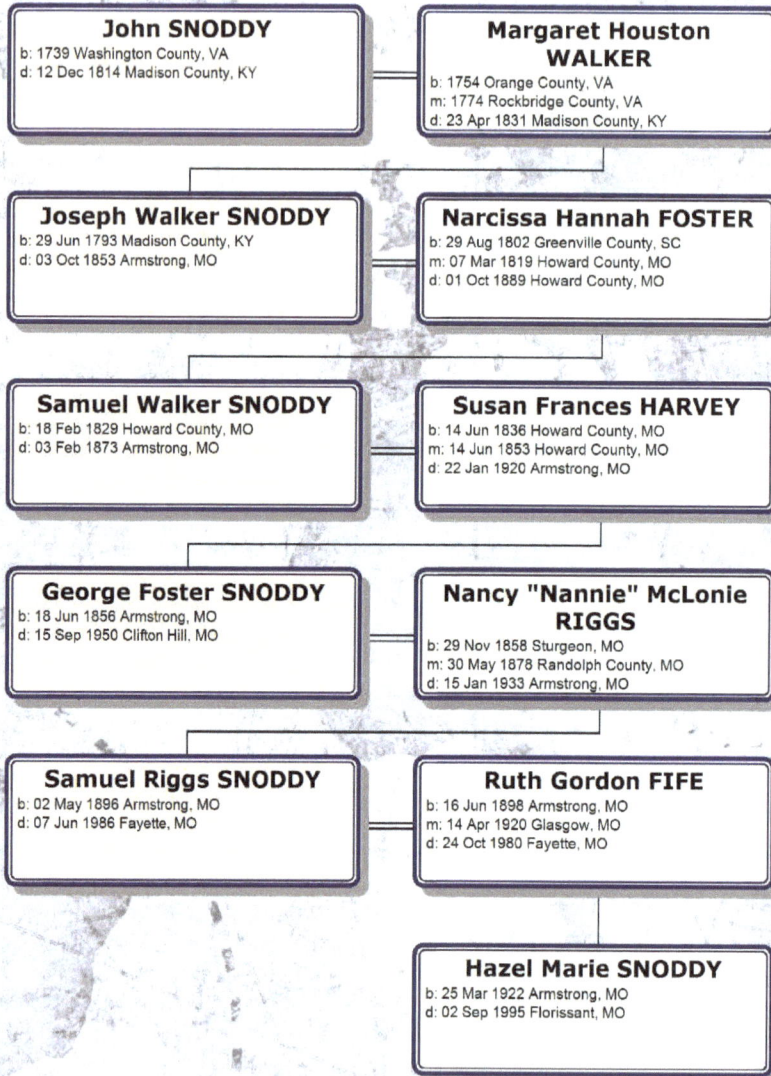

John SNODDY
b: 1739 Washington County, VA
d: 12 Dec 1814 Madison County, KY

Margaret Houston WALKER
b: 1754 Orange County, VA
m: 1774 Rockbridge County, VA
d: 23 Apr 1831 Madison County, KY

Joseph Walker SNODDY
b: 29 Jun 1793 Madison County, KY
d: 03 Oct 1853 Armstrong, MO

Narcissa Hannah FOSTER
b: 29 Aug 1802 Greenville County, SC
m: 07 Mar 1819 Howard County, MO
d: 01 Oct 1889 Howard County, MO

Samuel Walker SNODDY
b: 18 Feb 1829 Howard County, MO
d: 03 Feb 1873 Armstrong, MO

Susan Frances HARVEY
b: 14 Jun 1836 Howard County, MO
m: 14 Jun 1853 Howard County, MO
d: 22 Jan 1920 Armstrong, MO

George Foster SNODDY
b: 18 Jun 1856 Armstrong, MO
d: 15 Sep 1950 Clifton Hill, MO

Nancy "Nannie" McLonie RIGGS
b: 29 Nov 1858 Sturgeon, MO
m: 30 May 1878 Randolph County, MO
d: 15 Jan 1933 Armstrong, MO

Samuel Riggs SNODDY
b: 02 May 1896 Armstrong, MO
d: 07 Jun 1986 Fayette, MO

Ruth Gordon FIFE
b: 16 Jun 1898 Armstrong, MO
m: 14 Apr 1920 Glasgow, MO
d: 24 Oct 1980 Fayette, MO

Hazel Marie SNODDY
b: 25 Mar 1922 Armstrong, MO
d: 02 Sep 1995 Florissant, MO

End Notes

[1] Parke Rouse Jr., "The Saga of Castle's Woods," *The Great Wagon Road: from Philadelphia to the South* (New York: McGraw-Hill, 1973), 123-124.

[2] James W. Hagy, "The Frontier at Castle's Woods, 1769-1786," *The Virginia Magazine of History and Biography*, 75:4 (October 1967), 412, Virginia Historical Society.

[3] Emory L. Hamilton, "Frontier Forts," *Historical Sketches of Southwest Virginia* (Historical Society of Southwest Virginia, Publication 4, 1968), 3.

[4] Roberta Estes, "Logan's Lament," *Native Heritage Project*, 26 Jan 2014 (nativeheritageproject.com).

[5] "Wilderness Road," *History.com*, 12 Apr 2010, updated 21 Aug 2018.

[6] Hamilton, "Capt. John Snoddy Militia Officer," *Early Settlements of Wise County* (VaGenWeb).

[7] "Index of Militia Officers, 1777-1835," *The Militia of Washington County, Virginia* (Signal Mountain, Ind.: Mountain Press, 1979), 54.

[8] "Virginia Revolutionary War Service Records," Library of Virginia (lva-virginia.libguides.com).

[9] Hamilton, "Samuel Ritchie of Scott County, Virginia," *Historical Sketches of Southwest Virginia* (Historical Society of Southwest Virginia, Publication 12, 1978).

[10] David George Malgee, "A Frontier Biography: William Campbell of King's Mountain," Thesis, University of Richmond, August 1983, 61-62.

[11] Malgee, "A Frontier Biography," 72-73.

[12] Hagy, "The Frontier at Castle's Woods," 422.

[13] Hamilton, "Indian Tragedies Against the Walker Family" (RootsWeb.com).

[14] Ibid.

[15] "The American Revolution Revisited," *The Economist*, 29 Jun 2017.

[16] George C. MacKenzie, *King's Mountain*, National Military Park, South Carolina, (Washington, DC: National Park Service Historical Landmark Series 22, 1955), 26.

[17] "Court Minutes, vol. 1, 1777-1787," 106, Virginia. County Court, Washington County (FamilySearch.org).

[18] Workers of the Federal Writers Project of the Works Progress, G. Lee McLain, Military History of Kentucky, "I Sing of Arms and Men," *The Kentucky State Journal*, Frankfort, KY, 1939).

[19] Colonel John Snoddy, Indiana DAR, "Search for Revolutionary Era Ancestors."

[20] Walker Stewart. Unpublished manuscript, Garrard County Kentucky Historical Society, Lancaster, KY; John Snoddy (1739 - 1814) profile (WikiTree.com).

[21] "Celebrates Her 100th Birthday," *Moberly Monitor-Index*, Moberly, MO, 3 Aug 1936, 2 (Newspapers.com).

[22] Joseph Walker Snoddy memorial page (FindaGrave.com).

[23] Joseph Walker Snoddy land grants, "General Land Office Records, 1776-2015," Howard County, MO.

[24] Narcissa Hannah Foster Snoddy memorial page (FindaGrave.com).

[25] Tony O'Bryan, "Bushwhackers," *Civil War on the Western Border: The Missouri-Kansas Conflict, 1854-1865.* Kansas City Public Library. (civilwaronthewesternborder.org).

[26] George Foster Snoddy obituary, *Armstrong Herald*, Howard County, MO.; 15 Sep 1950.

[27] Bertha Snoddy tombstone, Snoddy-Garner Cemetery, Howard County, MO. (FindaGrave.com); "Miss Hazel Snoddy Dies Last Night," *Moberly Monitor-Index* (Moberly, MO), 9 Aug 1916, 7 (Newspapers.com).

James Milton Denny served with Kentucky mounted volunteers during the War of 1812 and fought at the Battle of the Thames. This print of a hand-colored 1833 lithograph by William Emmons depicts the death of Shawnee Chief Tecumseh at the battle. Col. Richard M. Johnson, leader of the Kentucky mounted volunteers, is in left foreground (Library of Congress)

From Frontiersman to Farmer

James Milton Denny

AT the dawn of the 19th century, Missouri frontier that became Howard County belonged to wildlife that inhabited forests, prairies and lowlands near the Missouri River. Though generally a quiet place, leaves fell and crackled underfoot and tree branches snapped as Native Americans made their way down hunting trails. Howling timber wolves and screaming panthers disturbed nights that they ruled.

That all began to change, slowly at first, then rapidly after Howard County organized in 1816. Many new settlers arrived, including James Milton Denny of Garrard County, Kentucky, who came in 1818 to claim land granted for service in the War of 1812. Hunters, trappers, explorers and other frontiersmen became the first English-speaking travelers to the area, but they had no intention of remaining permanently. Their interests centered on exploring this region and harvesting its bounty. Among early visitors, Nathan and Daniel M. Boone, sons of the famous explorer Daniel Boone, came in 1807 to process salt from many salt licks* in the area and ship it down the Missouri River to St. Louis for sale. From that point forward this region earned a nickname, "Boone's Lick Country."** Its first permanent settlement included 42 known families and possibly as many as 150 families. They settled during 1810 along Missouri River's Cooper's Bottom. Nearly two-thirds migrated from Madison County, Kentucky.[1] These included one-year-old Kit Carson, who left Howard County at age 17 and discovered a way to the Pacific Coast.

---

* Places where animals go to lick naturally occurring salt deposits.

** Destinations honoring Daniel Boone are inconsistent in spelling, i.e. Boone County, Boonville, Boonslick, Boonslick Trail, Boone's Lick Road, Boone's Lick Country and more.

Deer were plentiful in early Howard County and around the country during the 19ᵗʰ century. Here they find nighttime the right time to frolic. (George Siras, photographer; published in the 1906 National Geographic)

First settlers in Howard County found a land of plenty. Wild game furnished meat, including deer, prairie chickens, turkey, elk and bear. Deer could be seen daily, usually roaming in herds of 10 to 20, and sometimes as many as 50 grazed together. Settlers often considered it futile to grow crops, since small game such as squirrels and rabbits destroyed fields and gardens. Instead, they found it more productive to hunt and fish. Fur-bearing animals including otter, beaver, mink, muskrat, raccoon, panther, fox, wolf, wildcat and bear were abundant, providing warm clothing and bedding, as well as lucrative income from selling pelts. Timber wolves not only prowled at night, but could be seen during daylight, singly or in packs, lurking near thickets or moving warily along open paths. Trapping them became especially profitable after the state began paying a bounty for wolf scalps to reduce their numbers. Sometimes settlers paid taxes with wolf scalps. But rather than just thinning packs, timber wolves had disappeared from Missouri by the early 1900s.[2] Honeybees swarmed in great numbers near the Missouri River and in forests along various water courses in the county. During late summers, many settlers camped for days at a time to hunt and harvest wild bee honey, which brought high prices at markets. Nature also furnished almost everything necessary for early settlers' animals. Livestock grew fat on luxuriant grasses, nuts and berries. Even in winters, creatures pawed their way through snow and found grass.

Despite this bounty, further migration into the area slowed almost to a halt during the War of 1812. From 1812-1815 the war pitted United States forces against Great Britain, along with Native American allies on both sides. Though the Revolutionary War ended nearly 30 years earlier, animosity and greed continued between each country. Great Britain still tried to exercise control, including attempting to thwart United States efforts to become a maritime power. A British Royal Navy blockade limited trade with other countries. Warships confiscated merchant vessels and pressed American sailors into the Crown's service. Additionally, British leaders supported Native American efforts to prevent U.S. expansion into Old Northwest Territory bounded by the Ohio and Mississippi rivers This led to periodic bloody conflicts.

Lying near disputed territory, Kentucky provided the most U.S. forces to pursue war in the northwest. Major Gen. William Henry Harrison, then governor of Northwest Territory, had served for a time in the Kentucky Militia and relied on Kentucky for additional support. British Maj. Gen. Henry Proctor led opposing forces, along with Shawnee Chief Tecumseh, who put together a confederation of Native American tribes. Harrison considered Tecumseh a formidable foe. He stated in 1811, "The implicit obedience and respect which the followers of Tecumseh pay to him is really astonishing, and more than any other circumstances bespeaks him one of those uncommon geniuses which spring up occasionally to produce revolutions and overturn the order of things."[3]

After several major defeats at the hands of this British and Native American confederation, Kentuckians rose up to avenge fallen family members and friends. When Kentucky Gov. Isaac Shelby called for 1,500 volunteers to follow him into battle under Harrison's command, more than 4,000 men showed up. Recruits included Janes Milton Denny, age 23, who became part of Capt. Stephen Richardson's 6th Regiment of Mounted Kentucky Volunteers.[4]

An odd recruit joined as well. While this amassing force awaited orders at Newport, Kentucky, soldiers encountered two pigs fighting. When the female pig won this skirmish, they rewarded her with scraps of food, which became a daily ritual. Once soldiers began their march north, she followed them as far as the Ohio River, where the pig tried to board one of their rafts. The men shooed her off, assuming she would retreat and go home. Instead, the pig swam across the river and met up with them at their first camp. Impressed with her tenacity, troopers made this sow their mascot. She led a line of march each morning, but eventually tired out, fell behind and waddled into camp each evening squealing for supper.[5]

As Harrison's troops headed north, word came of a great American Naval victory on Lake Erie. It helped cut off supplies for British troops occupying Detroit and forced Proctor to retreat north up the Thames River. Their allied Native American confederation followed, though history records that Tecumseh became furious about not being consulted on this retreat. He called its British commander a "fat animal that carries its tail upon its back and when affrighted, it drops it between its legs and runs off."[6] On hearing news of their retreat, American forces penned up their horses and pig in a large pasture and ferried across Lake Erie after retaking Detroit. The troops, including James Milton Denny, then headed into Canada to confront Proctor's dispirited British soldiers and their unwavering allies led by Tecumseh. An ensuing Battle of the Thames, fought Oct. 5, 1813, became a rousing success for Americans. A defeated British commander fled the battlefield, while a proud Tecumseh fought until his death. Earlier the charismatic leader told his comrades to stand firm and fight to the end. He is reported to have said to his warriors, "Here, we will either defeat Harrison or leave our bones. This is a good place."[7]

Though a long march home should have been one of celebration for victorious Kentuckians, hardships followed them every step of the way. Exhausted men had fought a fierce battle, traveled 605 miles on horseback, 50 miles on water and 260 miles on foot – all in 65 days.[8] Their return also included little or nothing to eat and harsh weather, resulting in many illnesses and deaths. Troops stopped to pick up their horses and pig, and it might have made sense to eat the pig to help stave off starvation. Instead, the story is told that this pig received its own meager rations, and when she became weak from hunger, a wagon hauled her the rest of the way home. Kentucky Militia Pig, as they named her, was nursed back to health and lived out her days on Kentucky Governor Shelby's farm.

After troops arrived at Newport, Kentucky, in November 1813, James received an honorable discharge and returned to his family on Paint Lick Creek in Madison County, Kentucky. His father, Alexander Denny, had moved to Madison County in 1780 with his first wife, Mary Allison, where they acquired a 200-acre farm. Alexander was born in Frederick

Shawnee Chief Tecumseh
(Library of Congress)

County, Virginia, in 1747 to George Denny and an unknown spouse. George's early origins remain sketchy, but he may have come from Scotland to Virginia around 1720 with three brothers. George and his family later moved to Lincoln County, North Carolina, where he owned a 250-acre farm on Crowders Creek. Though too old to serve in the Revolutionary War, George's farm had supplied provisions for Patriot troops.

Like James's grandfather George, his father Alexander also was a Patriot whose farm provided food and other supplies to North Carolina, Virginia and South Carolina militias during the war's closing years. When James's wife Mary died, possibly during birth of their sixth child, he married Annie Clinton Adams in 1785, a widow with six young children of her own, and they had five additional children together. During 1818, Alexander and Annie and four of their adult children moved to the Boone's Lick area of Howard County, named for Gen. Benjamin Howard, Missouri's first territorial governor. With establishment of that county in 1816, government lands opened for settlement, including land grants from the War of 1812 for veterans such as the Dennys' son James. At that time, Howard County consisted of nearly 23,000 square miles, about one third as large as present-day Missouri. It became known as "Mother of Counties," since more than 40 counties were formed from portions of Howard. By 1825, its size had been reduced to 463 square miles. [9]

Like many others, Alexander and his family followed Boon's Lick Road, running from St. Charles westward and surveyed by Daniel Boone's sons in 1815. Extending east-west on the North side and roughly parallel to the Missouri River, it ended at Franklin in Howard County, where the Santa Fe Trail began.

The Missouri Intelligencer and Boon's Lick Advertiser noted this in its first publication on April 23, 1815:

> *The immigration to this territory, and particularly to this county, during the present season almost exceeds belief. Those who have arrived in this quarter are principally from Kentucky, Tennessee, etc. Immense numbers of wagons, carriages, carts, etc., with families, have for some time past been daily arriving. During the month of October it is stated that no less than 271 wagons and four-wheeled carriages and fifty-five two-wheeled carriages and carts passed near St. Charles, bound probably for Boon's Lick. It is calculated that the number of persons accompanying these wagons, etc., could not be less than three thousand. It is stated in the St. Louis Inquirer of the 10th instant that about twenty wagons, etc., per week had passed through St. Charles for the last nine or ten weeks, with wealthy and respectable immigrants from various states. Their united numbers are supposed to amount to twelve thousand. The county of Howard, already respectable in numbers, will soon possess a vast population, and no section of our country presents a fairer prospect to the immigrant.* [10]

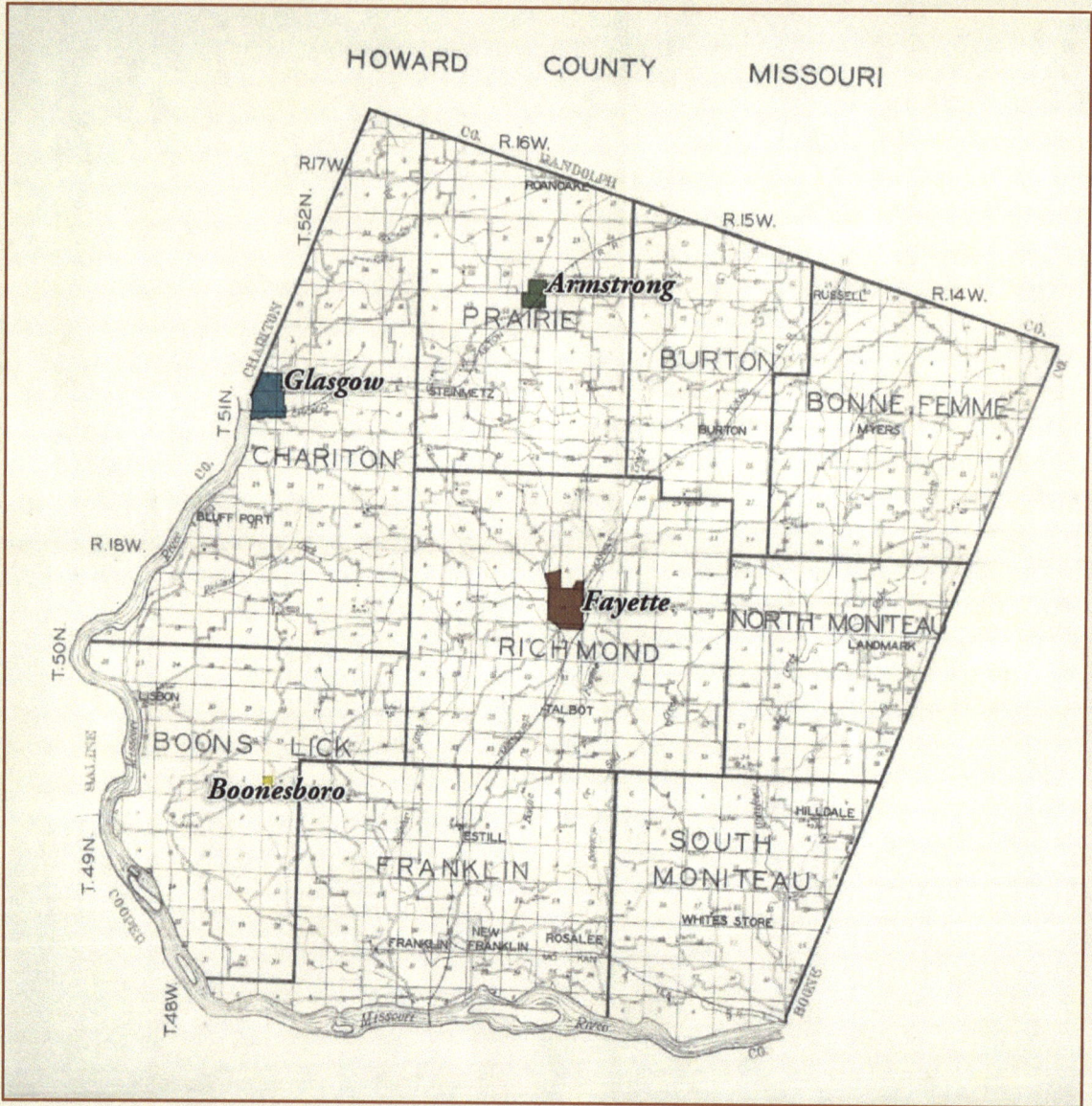

A 1930 Howard County Plat Book shows boundaries of the county after significant reductions from its original size. Key areas where Dennys and their kin settled include Fayette (county seat), Boonesboro, Glasgow and Armstrong. (State Historical Society of Missouri)

By the time Dennys arrived, Howard County had made great progress in organizing, even establishing a taxation rate through a circuit court:

> *Horse, mare, mule or ass above 3 years old: 25 cents*
>
> *Cattle above 3 years old: 6 ½ cents each*
>
> *Stud-horse, the sum for which he stands the season: 6 ¼ cents*
>
> *Billiard-table: $25*
>
> *Able-bodied single man of 21 years old or upwards not being possessed of property of the value of $200: 50 cents*
>
> *Water, gristmills, sawmills, horse mills, tan-yards and distilleries in actual operation: 40 cents on every $100 valuation.* [11]

Two years after migrating to Howard County, James married Elizabeth Best, born in Madison County, Kentucky, to Humphrey Best and Catherine Enyart. Elizabeth's father fought in the War of 1812 and also took advantage of land grant opportunities offered to veterans. Humphrey sold his Kentucky property and went to Missouri with his wife and children, including Elizabeth. Like other settlers, James and Elizabeth built a large two-story log structure where they reared 12 children. Missouri folks worked hard in homes and fields, but social gatherings with neighbors lessened their drudgery. Corn-husking parties and quilting bees provided opportunities for neighbors to get together. Settlers would sing and dance to fiddle contra tunes* such as Money Musk, Virginia Reel and Leather Britches.

For early Howard County residents, however, nothing equaled a spectacular phenomenon that occurred at about 4 a.m. on Nov. 13, 1833. A meteor storm of monumental proportions throughout the United States presented a majestic show in open skies above the Denny farm. Known as the Leonid Meteor Storm, innumerable balls of fire rushed across the sky, bursting like bombshells, and drawing long, luminous trains. Those awake at that hour watched with awe, along with fear and consternation, while between 50,000 and 150,000 meteors fell each hour. [12]

James managed to acquire a significant amount of land, beginning with a grant of 160 acres for war service. Later he acquired 90 acres from a nearby neighbor, 80 acres from a cousin and other acreages through about a dozen smaller land transactions. [13] An early description of agricultural land in Howard County depicted prairies covered with sweet, luxuriant grass equal to Kentucky's bluegrass. This likely attracted many Kentuckians. Rich sandy loam grew corn, wheat, oats and other cereal grains. The county also produced garden vegetables and orchard fruits.

In 1852 James built a large brick house between Armstrong and Glasgow that became

---

* Contra dance is a form of folk dancing made up of long lines of couples. It has mixed origins from English country, Scottish country, and French styles from the 17th century. A fiddle is the core instrument.

Home built west of Armstrong by James Milton Denny in 1852.

Home of Clifton E. and Mary Belle Denny, acquired in 1871. Later the home was inherited by their daughter and son-in-law, Leon and Cecile Denny Fife. The house remains in the Fife family.

a showplace in Howard County. Seven of his children occupied nearby farmsteads with equally magnificent houses. All were set back from the road and featured rolling bluegrass lawns, groves of trees, extensive outbuildings and abundant livestock and crops. An 1860 federal agricultural census, taken the year after his death, indicated 400 acres of land valued at $7,000 (about $259,000 today), producing primarily tobacco and livestock. For 12 months ending June 30, 1860, his farm yielded 8,000 pounds of tobacco, along with wheat, corn, oats, hay, flax and wool. His livestock, valued at $1,515, included horses, mules, milk cows, oxen, beef cattle, sheep and pigs.[14]

James's six sons and six daughters provided much of the labor for their farm and household. But James also worked eight enslaved people. These may have been one family, since records indicate a male, 36; a female, 35; and six others ranging from age 18 to age 2. At that time, enslaved labor performed much of the work on Howard County farms. By 1860, Howard exceeded every other county in the state in percentage of enslaved laborers – 37 percent.[15] It formed the heart of seven Missouri River counties known as Little Dixie for similarities shared with states in the upper and lower South, particularly slave-based production of hemp and tobacco.

Though James died in 1859, the year before the Civil War started, his family became deeply embroiled in this conflict. Three sons fought for the Union, including Alexander Denny, captain in a Federal Army Enrolled Militia. Two sons became Confederates, making it a war that tore families apart. And James's brother, Judge David Rice Denny, was hanged (though he survived) as a ploy to ambush the judge's son, Lt. Col. Alexander F. Denny. This Alexander commanded the 46th Regiment, Enrolled Missouri Militia, based at Huntsville, Missouri. He fought in several skirmishes against Confederate bushwhacker and murderer William T. "Bloody Bill" Anderson, who launched a plot to take Huntsville by luring militiamen out of that city. Anderson planned to accomplish this by going to the home of Alexander's elderly father, the judge, and hanging him from a gate post. Anderson then sent a servant into Huntsville to let Alexander know he had his father, thinking Alexander and his militia would rush there to save him. Townspeople, however, suspected it to be a trap and persuaded Alexander against going. When Bloody Bill realized that federal militia would not be lured into an ambush, he cut the judge down and left him for dead.

Confederate bushwhacker and murderer William T. "Bloody Bill" Anderson

According to local lore, Judge Denny crawled two miles into town. He suffered from complications for the remainder of his life.[16]

Clifton Enyart Denny, son of James Milton Denny, united with one of the best-known families of Howard County when he married a cousin, Mary Belle Enyart, after his Civil War service. Mary Belle's father, Humphrey Enyart, had a reputation as one of the most prosperous planters in this county. Her grandfather, Silas Enyart, joined the first wave of Kentuckians migrating to Howard County.

In 1871, not long after their marriage, Clifton and Mary Belle bought a house built by Uriah Pitts, possibly a Denny cousin. Pitts started building this house in 1840. He finished the dining room, with a sleeping loft above, and kitchen for the family to live in while finishing the remainder. It took 14 years to complete the two-story part of house. The date 1854 is inscribed on the cornerstone. Clifton and Mary Belle also inherited Enyart family land after the deaths of her parents. Eventually, Clifton amassed an estate of 750 acres, with portions of his land later acquired by his son-in-law, Leon Fife, and daughter Cecile Morgan Denny Fife. After Clifton's death in 1903, *The Armstrong Herald* remembered him as "one of the ablest farmers

of his vicinity and a citizen whose good works often extended beyond the boundaries of his family and household. The estate of seven hundred and fifty acres now occupied by Mrs. Denny has few superiors for comfort and productivity anywhere along the Missouri valley."[17]

Trying to sort out Dennys and their kin is like untangling thread. So many strands are knotted together that it is difficult to determine relationships. There are cousins who marry cousins, siblings in one family who marry siblings in another, and names repeated in every generation or even in the same generation. These close kinships resulted from being intertwined as neighbors and major landholders in Kentucky in the early 1800s.

Clifton Enyart Denny

Many pulled up stakes and moved to Howard County and environs between 1815 and 1820. Most pursued government land grants offered for service in the War of 1812. Some came from large families in search of land to settle. Others were drawn by reports of Howard County's beauty, fertile soil, navigable rivers and abundance of fish and game. Regardless of the reasons, Dennys and their kin came and made lasting contributions.

Clifton and Mary Belle Denny, along with more than 50 close kin, are buried in Walnut Hill Cemetery southwest of Armstrong, Missouri. The cemetery, on land donated by the Denny family, sits on a hill overlooking rich farmland.

Denny Direct Line

George DENNY
b: Abt. 1700 Great Britain or Ireland
d: 1788 Tryon County, NC

Alexander DENNY
b: 1747 Frederick County, VA
d: 05 Feb 1827 Armstrong, MO

Annie Clinton ADAMS
b: 1764 Lincoln County, KY
m: 10 Jun 1785 Paint Lick, KY
d: 14 Feb 1835 Armstrong, MO

James Milton DENNY
b: 01 Jan 1790 Paint Lick, KY
d: 20 Jan 1859 Howard County, MO

Elizabeth BEST
b: 23 May 1799 Madison County, KY
m: 02 Mar 1820 Bowling Green, MO
d: 03 Mar 1863 Howard County, MO

Clifton Enyart DENNY
b: 24 Jan 1842 Armstrong, MO
d: 05 May 1903 Armstrong, MO

Mary Belle ENYART
b: 30 Jan 1850 Armstrong, MO
m: 15 Oct 1865 Armstrong, MO
d: 17 Jun 1935 Tuscola, IL

Cecile Morgan DENNY
b: 20 Jun 1869 Armstrong, MO
d: 31 Aug 1966 Armstrong, MO

Leon Forest FIFE
b: 04 Oct 1869 Richmond, KY
m: 14 Feb 1891 Armstrong, MO
d: 22 Nov 1937 Armstrong, MO

Ruth Gordon FIFE
b: 16 Jun 1898 Armstrong, MO
d: 24 Oct 1980 Fayette, MO

Samuel Riggs SNODDY
b: 02 May 1896 Armstrong, MO
m: 14 Apr 1920 Glasgow, MO
d: 07 Jun 1986 Fayette, MO

Hazel Marie SNODDY
b: 25 Mar 1922 Armstrong, MO
d: 02 Sep 1995 Florissant, MO

End Notes

[1] Authentic official and private sources, *History of Howard and Cooper Counties, Missouri* (St. Louis: National Historical Co., 1883), 25, 93.

[2] "Gray [Timber] Wolves," *Missouri Department of Conservation* (mdc.mo.gov).

[3] Craig Baird, "Tecumseh," *Canadian History Ehx,* 13 Mar 2021 (canadaehx.com).

[4] James Milton Denny bounty application, "Bounty-Land Warrant Applications Index," Approved and disapproved bounty-land applications for soldiers who served post-Revolutionary War, 1790-1855 (Fold3.com).

[5] Doris Dearen Settles, *Kentucky and the War of 1812* (Charleston, SC: The History Press, 2023), 107-109.

[6] Baird, "Tecumseh."

[7] Ibid.

[8] Settles, *Kentucky and the War of 1812.*

[9] Walter Williams, ed., *A History of Northwest Missouri,* vol. I (Chicago: The Lewis Publishing Co., 1913), 352.

[10] Ibid., 5.

[11] *History of Howard and Cooper Counties,* 112.

[12] Malea Walker, "The 1833 Leonid Meteor Storm," *Library of Congress Blog,* 2 Sep 2020 (blogs.loc.gov).

[13] James Milton Denny land grants, 1 Apr 1825, "General Land Office Records, 1776-2015," Howard County, MO, Bureau of Land Management; "Howard County Deed Records, 1816-1924," vol. N-P 1832-1838; vol. 1-2 1850-1853 (FamilySearch.org).

[14] Elizabeth Denny, 1860 Agricultural Census, Glasgow, Chariton Township, Howard County, MO (sos.mo.gov).

[15] Stanley D. Maxson, "Up to freedom: slavery, emancipation, and the making of freedom in Howard County, Missouri, 1860 to 1865," master's thesis (Columbia: University of Missouri, 2015), 42.

[16] "Biographies: Alexander F. Denny," *Historic Huntsville, Missouri* (sites.google.com).

[17] Clifton E. Denny sketch, *Armstrong Herald,* "Pictorial and Biographical Edition, June 1896." Transcriptions donated to the Howard County MOGenWeb project by Betty Collier.

The 11th Kentucky Cavalry, led by John Hunt Morgan, storms through Washington, Ohio, during its 1863 raid of Ohio and Indiana. Not long thereafter, most of Morgan's raiders would be killed or captured, including Alex. (Hand-colored woodcut, North Wind Picture Archives)

Tunneling to Freedom

Dr. Alexander "Alex" Green Fife

On a bitter cold night in December 1863, with fog hiding the landscape, about 100 Confederate prisoners escaped from Camp Douglas on the outskirts of Chicago. They tunneled under their barracks, across the prison yard, beneath a fence and out to freedom. Alexander "Alex" Green Fife of Richmond, Kentucky, age 21, crawled with them. There would have been more escapees, except that as the fog lifted, a guard spotted men popping out of a hole beyond stockade walls. Prison officials recaptured most escapees, but Alex and others got away. Fate had other things in store for him, however, and he died less than eight years after his escape.

Alex's early life had been one of privilege. Born Oct. 9, 1842, to Alexander Fife and Mary Ross Green, he became the fifth of their six children who survived past childhood.[1] Raised on a horse farm in Madison County, Kentucky, just outside of Richmond, he had the best of everything, including private schooling at Madison Male Academy in Richmond, Kentucky. Afterward, Alex

pursued his interest in medicine by apprenticing with a doctor in the region. His father, also an Alexander, did not start with wealth. Born into a tenant farming family in Ardstraw Parish, County Tyrone, Ireland, he faced an uncertain future when mercenary landlords forced smaller leaseholders off the land by consolidating it into larger rental tracts. Alexander immigrated in 1824 and joined an acquaintance in a mercantile business in Lexington, Kentucky. His widowed mother, three brothers, and a sister remained in Ireland. Their letters to Alexander over many years provide evidence of a growing economic depression gripping the country.[2] His siblings vacillated on whether to join Alexander in America, but they were still in Ireland when potato crops failed in 1845. This plunged the country into a seven-year famine.

Alexander missed family and friends in his homeland, but eight years after his arrival in Kentucky he met and married the daughter of Daniel Green and Margaret Ross.[3] Green

Alexander Fife, father of Alex Green Fife, left his family in Ardstraw, County Tyrone, Ireland (depicted here), to make his way to America.

owned a quarter horse farm near Richmond, Kentucky, in Madison County and was an early settler in that region. At one time he owned more than 1,200 acres on the banks of Silver Creek and vicinity. Alexander's match made his mother happy back in Ireland, not because of the bride's wealthy family, but because they practiced the "right" religion. She extended blessings, noting in a letter, "We rejoice to think that tho far from us you did not intend to disgrace your freinds [sic] as your sweetheart you say is a Presbeterian [sic] and of a respectable family."[4]*

After Alexander's and Mary's marriage, he began acquiring land adjacent to his father-in-law's and went into the horse business as well. His holdings expanded in 1840 when the widowed Daniel Green died and left his daughter with 272 acres, his house, all household and kitchen furnishings and four slaves beyond ten already gifted to her. Green's remaining holdings went to Mary's two surviving brothers.[5] By the time Alexander died 20 years later he had enlarged his holdings considerably, leaving real estate valued at $15,000 ($832,200 in today's dollars) and personal property, including 25 slaves, valued at $13,000 ($750,920 today). One-third of the estate went to his wife and the remaining two-thirds were divided among six children, including Alex, not yet 18.[6]

Alex had no interest in farming, so he delegated operation of his share to his older brother, James. Alex continued preparations

---

* The surname "Fife" or "Fyffe" is spelled inconsistently by various members of the family.

for a medical career. But his plans took a detour one month shy of his 20th birthday, when the Civil War arrived at his doorstep. As a border state, Kentucky declared a neutrality policy at the beginning of the war. But Union and Confederate recruiters entered the state to enlist volunteers, and each side positioned troops on Kentucky's north and south borders. Both Union and Confederate militias mobilized within the state. By 1862, Unionists controlled the Kentucky legislature, while Southern sympathizers formed a shadow Confederate government. Ultimately 100,000 to 124,000 Kentuckians served in the Union Army. Between 25,000 and 40,000 Kentucky men joined Confederate troops.[7]

In August 1862, Gen. Kirby Smith's Confederate Army of Kentucky advanced toward Lexington as a first step in grand plans to make Kentucky a Confederate state. Just south of Alex's hometown of Richmond, about 6,850 Union soldiers, commanded by Gen. William "Bull" Nelson, clashed with 6,500 Confederate troops on August 30. Though fairly evenly matched in numbers, most Federals were raw recruits. Rebels whipped Union forces, leaving 4,900 Federal casualties, compared to about 750 Confederates.[8]

Rebels advanced north through the state for six weeks until they faced seasoned Federal troops, forcing them to retreat into Tennessee. Nevertheless, this Southern victory near Richmond whipped up fervor among young men with secessionist leanings. David Chenault, a prominent citizen of Madison County, began to recruit and organize a regiment from Madison and surrounding counties. Just 11 days after the Battle of Richmond, he formed the 11th Kentucky Cavalry with nine companies and 800 officers and enlisted men. Young Alex quit his medical studies, joined Company F as a corporal and received a $50 bounty for his three-year enlistment.[9]

Brig. Gen. John Hunt Morgan, a well-known Confederate raider operating in Kentucky, commanded the regiment. Though Morgan had no formal military training he achieved success using hit-and-run strikes to disrupt Union supply lines, divert Federal troops away from other campaigns and secure supplies for the Confederates. During a two-week raid at Christmas in December 1862, his men rode 400 miles into central Kentucky. They demolished 20 miles of railroad, destroyed an estimated $2 million worth of supplies and seized nearly 1,900 prisoners.[10]

For the first ten months, war seemed like a lark for Alex and his comrades, and the derring-do of Morgan's Raiders made them heroes among Confederate sympathizers. While ensconced at Monticello, Kentucky, during spring 1863, Alex assured his mother, "I'm enjoying myself fine with the warm county ladies. We have had one ball since we have been here, another to come off soon. . . . No telling when I will get home; need not be uneasy about me. I am doing very well."[11]

In July 1863 things changed. Morgan had been given carte blanche for raids throughout Kentucky, but General Braxton Bragg, regional Confederate commander, ordered him not to cross the Ohio River into Indiana and Ohio under any circumstances. Morgan ignored orders, however, and marched more than 2,400 men into Union territory. Only a few hundred men made it home from this unauthorized foray. Federals killed or captured the others. Chenault was killed in early July 1863, and most men in his 11th Kentucky Cavalry regiment were captured at Buffington's Island, Ohio, later the same month. Alex and others managed to retreat, but they became surrounded by a large Federal cavalry force and surrendered at Cheshire, Ohio. Federals sent these prisoners down the Ohio River, then took them by train to Camp Chase near Columbus. Their final destination – the infamous Camp Douglas in Chicago.

Referred to by many as "Andersonville of the North,"* Camp Douglas had a reputation as the worst of Union prisons, with unsanitary conditions, overcrowding, sparse rations and lack of bedding and clothing. Disease ran rampant, and death often trailed close behind. During the war Camp Douglas held about 26,000 prisoners, with a designated capacity of 6,000 to 7,000 at any given time. At one point, however, it contained 12,000 Confederates. An official death toll in the camp has been recorded at 4,039, though many fatalities went unreported. Some estimates place it between 5,000 and 6,000.[12]

Spectators crowded around the entrance to Camp Douglas to see the infamous Morgan's Raiders when they arrived during July and August 1863. *The Chicago Tribune* described these men as far better looking than any prisoners before them and the "character and daring of each individual as they passed could be guessed by his movements, and the quality of his 'store clothes.'" The newspaper also noted that "of the better dressed, more intelligent, sharp looking men, nearly all appeared contented, were laughing, joking, singing and whistling as they passed into their new prison quarters."[13]

Despite their carefree attitude going in, it did not last long amid onerous prison conditions. A Chicago medical inspection team called it "an extermination camp."[14] Nevertheless, along with performing chores assigned to them in camp, prisoners helped pass the time by writing letters, making rings and trinkets, playing cards, fielding sports teams, acting in skits, arguing, attending religious services and whatever else they could invent.

Punishments for offenses in camp ranged from humiliation to inflicting pain. For minor infractions prisoners might have to wear a box or barrel all day with their crime written on it, such as "For meddling in other people's business." Sometimes they had to stand on a small barrel all day or carry a ball and chain. A notorious punishment became known as "Morgan's Mule," which involved placing a narrow board across frames four feet or more above the floor and making prisoners ride this rail for hours while attempting to balance.[15]

During its 14 months of operation, Andersonville Prison in Georgia incarcerated 45,000 Union soldiers. Nearly 13,000 died from disease, poor sanitation, malnutrition, overcrowding or exposure.

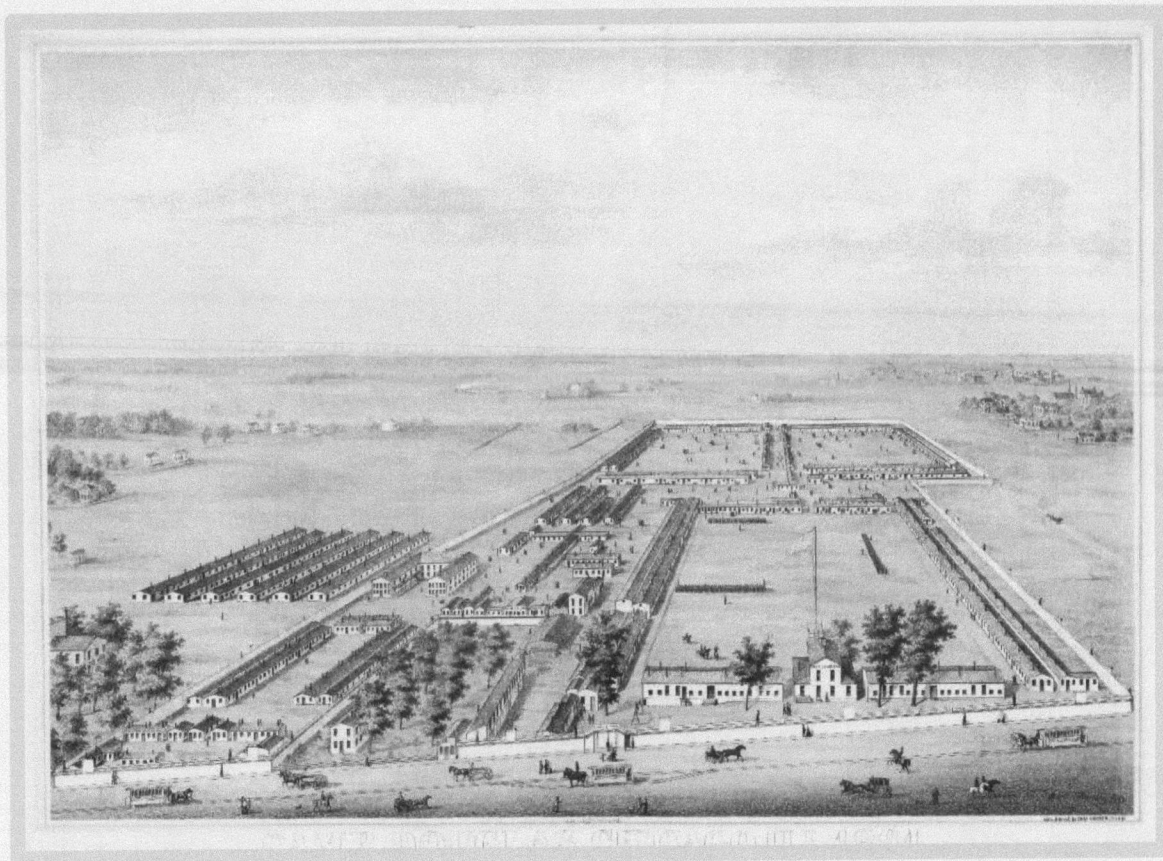

Depiction of Camp Douglas, Chicago, Illinois, 1864; established in Fall 1861. Area, 60 acres; strength of garrison, 1800; prisoners, 6000. View from Union Observatory. (Library of Congress)

Some of Morgan's men during imprisonment at Camp Douglas. Despite having 66 barracks, overcrowding at the prison sometimes swelled to as many as 12,000 prisoners. Outbuildings and kitchens also were used to house the overflow. (Harper's Weekly, *April 5, 1862*; True Williams)

Serious offences drew such punishments as hanging by the thumbs, being strung up by their heels and whipped, or sitting on snow and ice with bare buttocks during freezing temperatures. One of the most dreaded, however, was being thrown into White Oak Dungeon, an 18-square-foot room under a guard house with two air holes. When the door slammed shut the space became pitch black. Sometimes as many as 24 prisoners filled a room designed for no more than three or four men.[16] Escape attempts became common, though authorities foiled most at the outset or soon recaptured escapees. Some men burrowed tunnels under fences; others climbed over them, posed as workmen, or even walked through front gates after bribing guards. Kentucky kinsmen sometimes aided them. Along with bribery, friends slipped cryptic notes past guards, mothers sewed contraband inside clothing, fathers sent messages about weak points on the prison perimeter, and young ladies prepared cakes for their beaus with rendezvous locations inside. Some even sent breezy messages about family and friends with coded information written between lines in invisible ink.

An article in the Nov. 4, 1863, *Louisville Daily Journal* in Kentucky lamented after a foiled escape attempt in October 1863:

> The plot laid for the escape of rebel prisoners has cost the wealthy Kentuckians weeks of hard study, hundreds of dollars-- not only in the amount of their hotel bills, and the expense of daily travelling to Camp Douglas and back, for weeks at a time, but it is known that outside parties had been liberally paid to do their dirty work, before they paid the $1,200 bribe to the guards.

Some escapees were caught because they lingered in Chicago too long. Rather than put a substantial distance between them and Camp Douglas, they could not resist drinking and carousing at downtown establishments. Some brazen ones took other unnecessary risks. An escapee told a newspaper reporter that he and other fugitives hired a hack driver to take them to the train station. When he overcharged them, they filed a complaint with police and stayed overnight to testify in court the next day. The hack driver was fined $10 and had to refund half of his charge to each.[17]

The most audacious escape occurred at night on December 2, 1863, when Alex and approximately 80 to 100 comrades tunneled out of Barracks No. 3. Authorities soon recaptured all but about 20, with Alex managing to avoid detection. Two days after this escape the prison sought help from the public in finding those still at large. They described Alex as 5'7" with blue eyes, red hair, and a fair complexion. (Actually, his enlistment record indicated dark hair and dark eyes.) But

This muster roll documents Alexander Fife's escape (National Archives)

the plea failed.[18] In his official report, camp commandant Charles V. De Land noted that "foggy weather shrouded the camp on the night of their breakout, so guards were on patrol outside the stockade. Nevertheless," he conceded, "prisoners poured through the tunnel from 8:00 p.m. to 9:30 p.m."[19] The unlighted fence and the dark prison yard contributed to their success.

One of the most detailed escape reports appeared in a *Louisville Daily Journal* on Dec. 10, 1863, apparently told to a reporter by a prisoner involved:

> "The means of their escape was traced to the northeast corner of a small room in the barracks No. 3. The room is about

eight feet square, and contains a cooking stove, bunk, etc. The bunk was covered with straw and was elevated about one foot from the floor. The straw had been thrown back, and two or three of the boards removed from the bottom of the bunk -- which gave them access to the floor, through which they cut an opening sufficiently large to allow them to commence operations in the ground. A hole from four to six feet in depth was then dug, which was good enough in circumference to allow a man to work with ease. From this excavation the prisoners constructed a tunnel four feet below the surface of the ground, and large [enough] that they could pass along its extent without hindrance. Their point of egress was fifty-seven feet and three inches distant from the room where their escape commenced and was just outside the fence which encloses the camp. They seemed to have calculated the distance with mathematical precision, while their work was conducted with the utmost secrecy and caution. The ground above the line of the tunnel did not afford the least evidence of what was going on below. The earth which the prisoners had removed was carried back and carefully concealed beneath the kitchen under which they had to pass."

Curtis Burke, one of Morgan's men who did not participate in this breakout, noted that "had they come up two feet back they would have been seen by the guard. The Yankees were so mad that they came around and tore down all of the partitions and throwing all of the little rooms into one big room in each barrack. . . . Col. De Land said that he would turn us all out in the weather if we did not quit digging out."[20] Those who remained in camp paid dearly for this escape. Guards tore out floorboards in each barrack and packed spaces between joists with dirt, meaning bunks sat on the ground. No barrier protected prisoners from Arctic blasts that blew in later that month with heavy snow, gale force winds and sub-zero temperatures. Guards took away bedding and warm clothing. For a time, prisoners had to strip naked before going outside to the latrine at night, regardless of the weather. Chicago

Long Island College Hospital, where Alex Fife received his medical degree in 1865. (College circular and catalogue for 1966 session)

newspapers remained full of stories and speculation about the escape. Most believed escapees had help from outsiders -- namely friends and relatives from Kentucky. According to newspapers, a build-up of Kentuckians reserving rooms in Chicago hotels and lurking around prison walls had been noted for days. Further, many recaptured men, including some only hours after their escape, wore new suits of clothes and had money in their pockets. Escape of Morgan's men and others caused former Confederate prisoner Henry Lane Stone to reflect on it long after the war, "The same restless, daring spirit that actuated Morgan's men in the field characterized them in prison. . . I have heard that one of the Chicago newspapers stated during the war that even if Morgan's men had done nothing to distinguish them before their capture on the raid through Indiana and Ohio, they had immortalized themselves by their wonderfully successful escapes from prison." [21]

What happened to Alex immediately after his escape is unknown. But it is substantiated that he had resurfaced by March 1865 as a student at Long Island College Hospital in Brooklyn, New York, where he graduated in July 1865. [22] Southerners who wished to become doctors often attended northern medical schools, and the Civil War seemed to be no barrier. Some Southerners continued in northern schools throughout the war, and physicians exchanged letters across the Mason-Dixon Line to maintain professional relationships. [23] In those days medical degrees required three-year apprenticeships with a practicing physician (called a preemptor), plus completion of two, 16-week terms of lectures at a chartered medical college. Faculty typically gave the same lectures each term, so Alex likely followed a tradition of taking his first term elsewhere to avoid repetitive classes. [24] He may have completed some or all of his three-year-apprenticeship before entering the war. But possibly Alex received credit for assisting Confederate surgeons in Camp Douglas prison. While Union doctors served in the camp, they primarily aided Federal troops

Dr. Alex Fife

Oil portrait ca. 1868-1870.
(Photographic image by
Notley Hawkins)

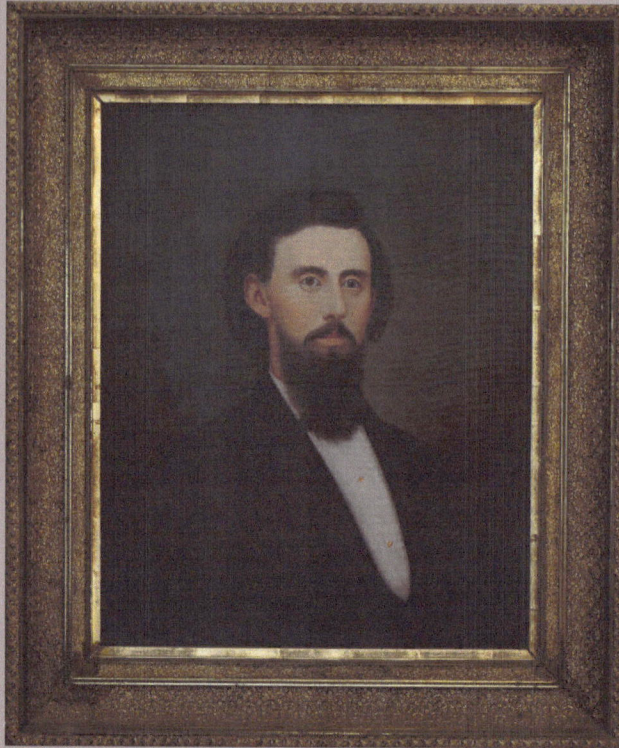

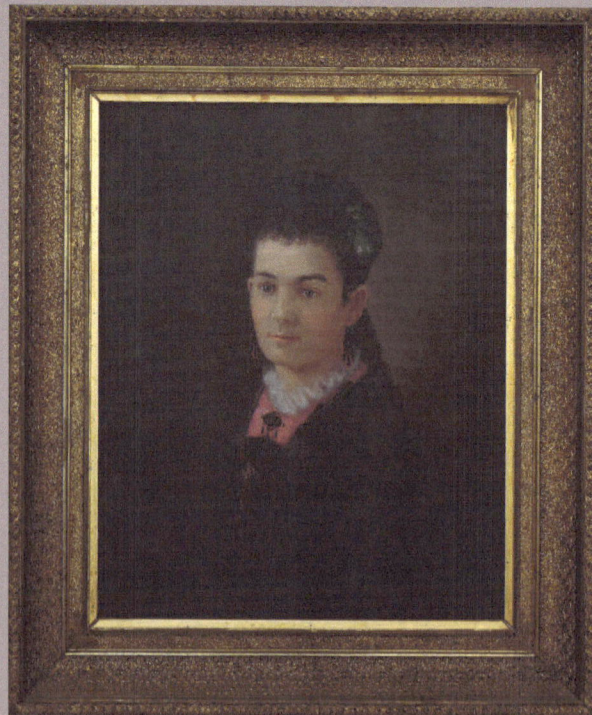

Annie Turner Fife

Oil portrait ca. 1868-1870.
(Photographic image by
Notley Hawkins)

garrisoned there. Confederate surgeons typically cared for fellow prisoners, assisted by other inmates with some degree of medical training or interest. Alex returned to Madison County, Kentucky, after graduation to set up his medical practice, and early in 1869 he married Annie Turner, daughter of Alfred Turner and Martha White. Their only child, Leon Forest Fife, was born later that year, but Alex died three weeks before his 29th birthday and his son's second birthday.[25] While riding his horse at a gallop enroute to tend to a patient, he struck a tree limb, breaking his neck. It seems odd that a boy who grew up on a horse farm and rode with Morgan's Cavalry during the Civil War would be killed by a horse. His widow and young son lived with various relatives in Madison County while Leon grew up. After completing his education at Central University in Richmond, Kentucky, he migrated to Missouri at age 21 in search of new opportunities, like his grandfather Alexander who came from Ireland to start a new life in Kentucky. Two of his mother's brothers lived in Browning, Missouri, where they had a mercantile business and agreed to employ him.

Finding this business unsatisfactory, Leon decided to try his hand at farming in Howard County and won the hand of Cecile Morgan Denny as well. Again, like his grandfather before him, he married into a long-time pioneering family of some wealth. Her father gifted them 130 acres, though somewhat skeptical of his new son-in-law's farming abilities. Leon surprised them all by becoming a successful farmer in the county, eventually amassing about 500 acres. Cecile's mother moved into town after the death of her husband and sold the Denny farmstead to her daughter and son-in-law, adding to his acreage.[26] Like the Fifes, the Dennys had been slaveholders. When Leon and Cecile moved into the homeplace in 1904, remnants of slave quarters remained, though they used them to store crop materials and farming equipment. The family lived out their lives on the farm. It included four daughters and two sons, along with Leon's widowed mother, Annie Turner Fife, who moved from Kentucky.[27] She brought with her two cherished oil portraits, Alex and Annie, painted around the time of their marriage.

Leon's grandfather experienced what it was like to be treated unfairly as a tenant farmer in Ireland. His father knew what it meant to be a prisoner stripped of freedom and dignity. And Leon faced hardships in growing up without a father. Each of them impart lessons about man's inhumanity to man and triumph of the human spirit.

Leon Forest Fife and Cecile Denny Fife, ca.1935

Fife Direct Line

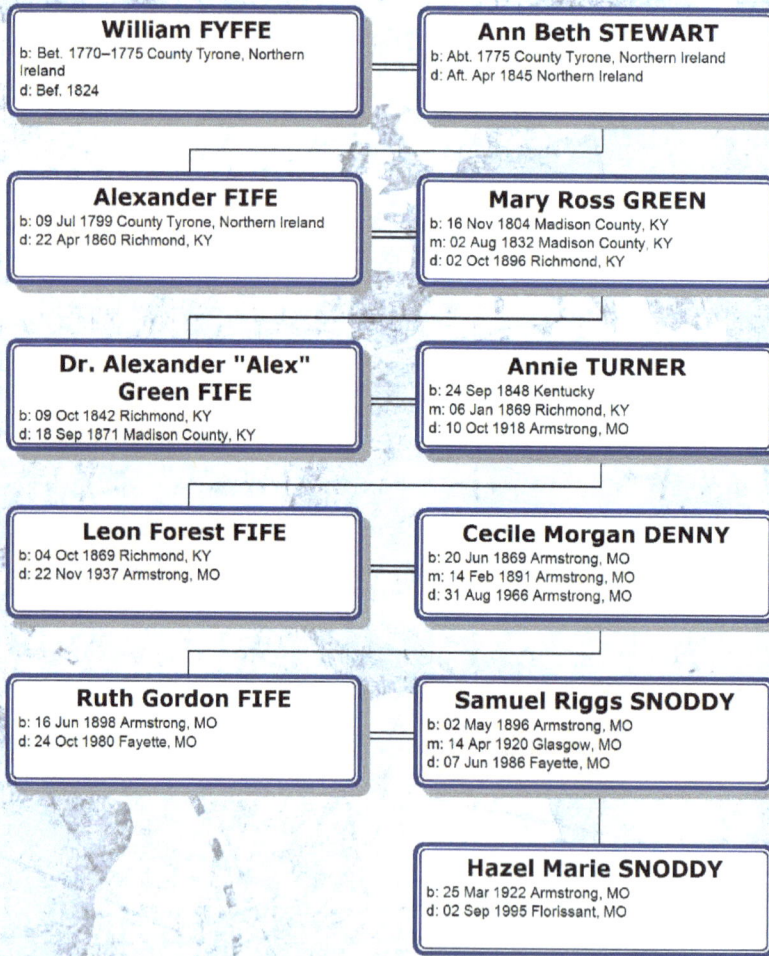

William FYFFE
b: Bet. 1770–1775 County Tyrone, Northern Ireland
d: Bef. 1824

Ann Beth STEWART
b: Abt. 1775 County Tyrone, Northern Ireland
d: Aft. Apr 1845 Northern Ireland

Alexander FIFE
b: 09 Jul 1799 County Tyrone, Northern Ireland
d: 22 Apr 1860 Richmond, KY

Mary Ross GREEN
b: 16 Nov 1804 Madison County, KY
m: 02 Aug 1832 Madison County, KY
d: 02 Oct 1896 Richmond, KY

Dr. Alexander "Alex" Green FIFE
b: 09 Oct 1842 Richmond, KY
d: 18 Sep 1871 Madison County, KY

Annie TURNER
b: 24 Sep 1848 Kentucky
m: 06 Jan 1869 Richmond, KY
d: 10 Oct 1918 Armstrong, MO

Leon Forest FIFE
b: 04 Oct 1869 Richmond, KY
d: 22 Nov 1937 Armstrong, MO

Cecile Morgan DENNY
b: 20 Jun 1869 Armstrong, MO
m: 14 Feb 1891 Armstrong, MO
d: 31 Aug 1966 Armstrong, MO

Ruth Gordon FIFE
b: 16 Jun 1898 Armstrong, MO
d: 24 Oct 1980 Fayette, MO

Samuel Riggs SNODDY
b: 02 May 1896 Armstrong, MO
m: 14 Apr 1920 Glasgow, MO
d: 07 Jun 1986 Fayette, MO

Hazel Marie SNODDY
b: 25 Mar 1922 Armstrong, MO
d: 02 Sep 1995 Florissant, MO

End Notes

[1] 1850 U. S. Census, Madison County, KY, Alexander Fife household (Ancestry.com).

[2] *Green/Fife/White Family Papers, 1797-1955*, Special Collections and Archives, Eastern Kentucky University, Richmond, KY.

[3] Alexander Fife-Mary Ross Green marriage certification, Kentucky Marriages, Madison County Courthouse, Richmond, KY (Ancestry.com).

[4] "Letter from Ann Fife to Alexander Fife, March 26, 1832," *Green/Fife/White Family Papers.*

[5] Daniel Green will, "Kentucky Probate Records, 1727-1990," Madison County Kentucky Courthouse, Wills, vol. G, 278-280.

[6] Alexander Fife probate records, 1860-1862, Madison County Kentucky Courthouse, vol. 0-S (FamilySearch.com).

[7] Garry Adelman, "A House Divided: Civil War Kentucky" *American Battlefield Trust* and Mary Bays Woodside, *Hallowed Ground Magazine*, 16 Apr 2010, updated 21 Dec 2021.

[8] American Battlefield Trust, Battle of Richmond (battlefields.org).

[9] Alexander Green Fife, "Military Service Records, 1862-63" (Fold3.com).

[10] Garry Adelman, "A House Divided."

[11] Letter from Alexander Green Fife to Mary Ross Fife, 8 Apr 1863, *Green/Fife/White Family Papers.*

[12] David L. Keller, "Camp Douglas September 1861-December 1865: (A Chicago story that must be told)," Camp Douglas Restoration Foundation, December 2013 (CampDouglas.org); Joseph L. Eisendrath, Jr., "Chicago's Camp Douglas, 1861-1865," *Journal of the Illinois State Historical Society.* 53:1 (Spring 1960), 37-63.

[13] *Chicago Tribune*, Chicago, IL, 19 Aug 1863, 4 (Newspapers.com).

[14] *The War of the Rebellion: a Compilation of the Official Records of the Union and Confederate Armies*, Series 2, vol. 5, 588 (babel.hathitrust.org).

[15] George Levy, *To Die in Chicago: Confederate Prisoners at Camp Douglas 1862-1865* (Gretna, LA: Pelican Publishing Co., 1999), 203.

[16] Lonnie R. Speer, *Portals to hell : military prisons of the Civil War* (Mechanicsburg, PA: Stackpole Books, 1997), 181-182.

[17] *The Louisville Daily Journal* (Louisville, KY), 4 Nov 1863, 1.

[18] *Chicago Tribune*, Chicago, IL, 4 Dec 1863, 4; (Newspapers.com).

[19] George Levy, *To Die in Chicago*, 164-165.

[20] "Curtis R. Burke Civil War Journal," ed. Pamela J. Bennett, *Indiana Magazine of History*, 66:2 (June 1970), 132-133.

[21] Henry Lane Stone, *Morgan's Men: Narrative of Personal Experience.* Presentation to George B. Eastin Camp, No. 803, United Confederate Veterans, 8 Apr 1919 (Louisville, KY: Westerfield-Bonte Co, 1919), 23.

[22] Alexander Green Fife, "Circular and Catalogue of the Long Island College Hospital: Session for 1866" (Brooklyn: "The Union" Steam Presses, 1965) 7-8. (Ancestry.com).

[23] Natalie Shibley, "Race and Early American Medical Schools: Review of Christopher D.E. Willoughby's Masters of Health: Racial Science and Slavery in U.S. Medical Schools," *Clio Reads*, 14 Feb 2023 (NursingClio.org).

[24] Downstate Medical Center Alumni Association, *History of the Long Island College Hospital, Long Island College of Medicine, and the State University of New York College of Medicine at New York City,* New York, 1961, 15. (archive.org).

[25] Alexander Green Fife-Annie Turner marriage, "Kentucky Marriages," Madison County Courthouse, Richmond, KY (Ancestry.com); "Distressing and Fatal Accident," *The Tri-Weekly Maysville Eagle,* Maysville, KY, 28 Sep 1871; Alexander Green Fife tombstone (FindaGrave.com).

[26] Leon F. Fife, "A Leading Howard Countian;" 1920 U. S. Census, Mary Belle Enyart Denny household, Armstrong, Howard County, MO (Ancestry.com).

[27] 1910 U.S. Census, Leon F. Fife household, Howard County, MO (Ancestry.com).

St. Louis officially became an American city after ceremonies transferred it from Spain to France at noon on March 9, 1804, then from France to the United States at noon on March 10, 1804. Though Spain had secretly given Upper Louisiana (including St. Louis) back to France, ownership had to be recognized before the Louisiana Purchase of 1803 could be validated. This is one of many depictions of raising the American flag over St. Louis and lowering the French flag. (Postcard after F. L. Stoddard, Missouri History Museum, Photograph and Print Collection)

In a Foreign Land

Vincent Carrico

Vincent Carrico and Susannah Quick birthed their older children in a kingdom, their middle children in an empire, and their youngest children in a territory. Yet they lived their entire married life in the Spanish Lake area of St. Ferdinand Township, part of what became St. Louis County, Missouri. Vincent and Susannah arrived from Kentucky not long after their 1796 marriage. This region west of the Mississippi River had experienced constant turmoil thanks to major powers attempting to expand. Spain owned the land at the time, having taken it in 1770 from France, which wrested it from Native Americans.

Born around 1765 in Bryantown Hundred, Maryland, Vincent was too young to care about Spanish takeover of a territory that then seemed far away. His grandfather, Peter Carrico, had arrived in Colonial Maryland from France in the early 1700s.* He owned and farmed two tracts of land: Maidstone acquired through his first wife and Carrico's Hope** purchased after his marriage to Margaret Gates. Vincent's father, James, inherited Carrico's Hope, after Peter's death. There James raised 13 children with his wife, Elizabeth Clement, whose roots went back to the second Lord Baltimore, governor of Maryland, as well as royalty in England.

Their oldest son, Vincent, did not remain in Maryland. Instead, he set out for new experiences and an opportunity to acquire his own farmland, rather than share a divided interest with his siblings after his father's death. He joined countless others following the Great Wagon Road, which reached Roanoke, Virginia, before branching off to the

* Though Peter's origins are not confirmed, descendants note that "Carrico" comes from the French "Carriceau" or "Carricoits," and early Carrico ancestors spoke French.
** Maryland attached legal names to property until the 18th century. Titles might be descriptive such as The Cow Pasture, reflect names of places left behind in the old country such as Maidstone, or address colonists' dreams such as Carrico's Hope.

Vincent Carrico's father, James, and grandfather, Peter, farmed primarily tobacco and Indian corn on their Maidstone and Carrico's Hope land in Maryland. As depicted in this historic re-creation of tobacco cultivation, both men and women worked in the fields. (Sydney E. King, Colonial National Historical Park, National Park Service)

Wilderness Trail carved out by Daniel Boone. That trail took settlers through the Cumberland Gap into Kentucky.

Enroute to Kentucky, Vincent met and married Fanny Estes, daughter of Elisha Estes, during 1791 in Franklin County, Virginia. It is unclear what happened to Fanny because in 1796 Vincent married Susannah Quick in Madison County, Kentucky. After this second marriage Vincent and Susannah moved with other Kentuckians to Upper Louisiana territory governed by Spain. Spain had installed a colonial government within a few years of acquiring its new land from France, but when the Carricos arrived more than 25 years later it remained sparsely populated. St. Louis and smaller settlements that grew up around it were largely French Creole.* The few Spaniards living there had come primarily because Spain sent them to occupy government positions. Despite Spanish rule, French culture continued to permeate business dealings, social interactions and events such as weddings, christenings and funerals. Many place names and customs in St Ferdinand Township and nearby areas reflect French influences.[1]

Spanish governors lacked enthusiasm for America's westward immigration into Upper Louisiana, but onset of the Anglo-Spanish War in 1796 changed that. Spain needed an influx of new residents to help defend this region. Assuming Americans retained animosity toward England after declaring their

---

* *French Creole were those of French ancestry born in colonial French territories outside of France.*

independence, the Spanish government began to recruit them. Newspapers in nearby states advertised free land of 1,000 arpents (about 840 acres) at an Upper Louisiana location of the settlers' choosing and almost free of subsequent taxes if they paid fees and survey expenses.[2] Vincent, then living in Madison County, Kentucky, joined those who responded, along with other Kentuckians such as Daniel Boone.

The large Kentucky response stemmed partly from Kentucky land policy abuses at the time. Law on the frontier allowed vague and ill-defined land entries, leading to overlapping claims and other problems. Surveys could not be cross-checked to determine if prior claims existed. Speculators made only minimal improvements to land, sometimes just cutting and piling up logs for a cabin, then selling it for whatever they could get. Unscrupulous sales to more than one person caused legitimate claims to be questioned.

Beginning their married life in Spanish-held territory, where terms of land grants were clearly spelled out, appealed to Vincent and Susannah. Susannah's parents, Benjamin and Lydia Lovett Quick, joined them in this relocation. Vincent staked his claim on a high

Though controlled by Spain during the last part of the 18th century, St. Louis remained decidedly French in language, customs and daily life. This drawing depicts life in colonial St. Louis and across the river in Illinois. (Missouri History Museum)

bluff overlooking the confluence of the Missouri and Mississippi rivers. His 1,000-arpent grant was in an area known as Spanish Pond, or Spanish Lake, and a mile from Fort Belle Fontaine.[3] The fort, then a primitive Spanish military and trading post, became an important gathering place for soldiers, Native Americans, trappers and traders, along with French, Spanish and American settlers.

Early in Spain's régime, settlers had to swear allegiance to both King and Catholic Church to be allowed into this region. Later, when Spain began recruiting settlers, authorities admitted Protestants. But Spanish law did not allow practice of their religion, and their children had to receive Catholic baptism. Vincent and Susannah, both Catholics, had their 11 children baptized in St. Ferdinand Catholic Church. However, they had some Protestant kinsmen. One of Vincent's relatives helped establish the first Protestant services in this region. Abraham Musick, whose son Reuben married Vincent's daughter Lydia, had a friend who was a Baptist minister in Illinois. His friend, Reverend John Clark, frequently crossed the river for religious discussions with Musick and his neighbors. This led Musick to request an exception from Commandant Zénon Trudeau to enable Clark to preach in Musick's home. Though favorable to American settlers and a close friend of Musick, Trudeau rejected this petition, stating, "No, Monsieur Musick, I can not permit no such ting; tis against de law. You must all be bon Catholique in dis countree." Discouraged, Musick rose to leave Trudeau's office, but the commandant told him to sit back down. He added that Musick could not put a cross or a bell on his house and call it a church. Nor could Clark baptize anyone. "But if your friend come to see you, your neighbor come there, you conversez; you say prayer; you read Bible; you sing song -- dat is all right -- you all bon Catholique."[4]

Clark visited Musick's house every month. But to give an appearance of enforcing Spanish law, Trudeau kept track of Clark's visiting schedule. Two or three days before Clark's planned return to Illinois, the commandant would send a threatening message that if Clark did not leave Spanish country within three days he would be imprisoned. Thus, while he did not give legal sanction to visits of a preacher from another denomination, he gave Clark ample time to complete his ministry and retreat across the river. Much later Clark's congregation began meeting in John Patterson's house, forming the nucleus for Cold Water Baptist Church (located near Cold Water Creek). It became a forerunner of Salem Baptist Church attended by Carrico extended families through modern times. The congregation chose Salem, a Biblical word for "peace," when its congregation split over slavery.[5]

Spanish control of Upper Louisiana lasted just 30 years before Spain gave up its goal of becoming a major power in this region. Spain secretly ceded the land back to France in 1800,[6] though Spain continued as administrative agent until 1803. At that time, Spain had to officially cede the territory to

This early map of the Spanish Lake area of St. Louis County shows Vincent's original Spanish land grant (Survey 52). Later he and other Carricos acquired additional land around them.

France before France could sell it to the United States as part of the Louisiana Purchase. Ceremonies in St. Louis called for lowering the Spanish flag and flying the French flag for several hours before lowering it and hoisting the American flag. However, St. Louisans of French origin were so happy to see their flag flying that officials agreed to keep it up for a full 24 hours before raising the Stars and Stripes.

With official land grants now issued in a different country, grantees such as Vincent had to confirm their ownership through a new government. In 1805 Congress passed an act that all warrants obtained from French or Spanish governments must be confirmed no later than March 1, 1806, or become void. Claimants had to present proof that they inhabited and cultivated their land prior to October 1, 1800. Squatters without grants who had been living on and cultivating their farms before 1800 also could make claims.[7] Officials validated Vincent's claim, but for many, including Daniel Boone, it became a contentious process that often took years to resolve.

Land began changing hands when previous land grants were forfeited or sold by original owners. Several of Vincent's siblings, including Walter, Dennis, Theresa and Elizabeth, also arrived from Kentucky to acquire land. This expanded Carrico influence in St. Ferdinand Township. Children in each Carrico branch intermarried with other pioneers, including Pattersons, Humes, Musicks, Warrens, St. Vrains, Fugates, Martins and more, making it a tight-knit community. Carricos also married

among themselves. Vincent's son Daniel returned briefly to Kentucky where he married 15-year-old Matilda Carrico, daughter of Vincent's brother Walter. Their marriage required written permission from her parents, likely due to her age as well as a first cousin relationship. Daniel and his bride returned to Missouri with an entire branch of her family. Matilda died just three years after their wedding, leaving a two-year-old son, James Walter, called Walter after her father.

Following the Louisiana Purchase, Fort Belle Fontaine near the Carrico property became a starting point for many exploratory expeditions to the American West. Among them, the Lewis and Clark party camped on a nearby island shortly after setting off from Camp River Dubois in Illinois during 1804. They also stayed at the newly completed Fort Belle Fontaine on the last night of their return trip in 1806. Built in 1805, it became the first U.S. military installation west of the Mississippi River. Builders located this fort on Missouri River's south bank, near Cold Water Creek's mouth and close to its Mississippi River confluence. Later a shift in Missouri River's channel swept away the post, and a new fort replaced it.

Though most Carricos engaged in agriculture, Vincent's daughter Lydia and her husband, Reuben Musick, bought Hall's Ferry, known as Musick's Ferry after their purchase. An adjacent Musick's Inn primarily housed men who came across the Missouri River at St. Charles to sell wares in St. Louis. The inn also provided great entertainment for St. Louis County residents, with showboats docking

Musick's Ferry and Inn were owned by Vincent Carrico's daughter Lydia and her husband, Reuben Musick. After acquiring the ferry in 1848, they began construction on the inn (pictured here) to accommodate customers. The inn had walls nearly two feet thick. While it no longer exists, photos were taken in 1933 as part of the Historic American Buildings Survey. (Library of Congress)

regularly. Some believe the ferry was a stop on the Underground Railroad, which sneaked black freedom seekers across the Missouri River to St. Charles, then on to the free state of Illinois.[8]

During his lifetime Vincent amassed more than 3,000 acres of rich farmland by buying up land grants and parcels of land in Spanish Lake and adjacent Old Jamestown areas in St. Ferdinand Township. To partially finance his Missouri landholdings, he sold off tracts of land inherited when his father, James, died during December 1799 in Maryland. Maryland deeds indicate that Vincent resided in "New Spain in the Upper Louisiana."[9] In 1803 Vincent also purchased four slaves from

his late father's estate. Like many neighbors who came from Kentucky, Vincent relied on enslaved labor to cultivate his land. When he died in 1816, Vincent's will left 400 acres of land to his wife, with the remainder divided among 11 children. He bequeathed his enslaved laborers Ally and Abram to his wife, while setting free his long-time servant, Willis. All other enslaved laborers were to be rented out, with proceeds going into a trust for schooling his minor children or equally divided when all became of age.[10]

When Vincent arrived in 1796 a Spanish colonial census reported seven enslaved people in St. Ferdinand Township. By 1800, shortly before Louisiana Territory became part of the United States, that number had reached 17.[11] It continued to grow as settlers placed more land into production. Before the Civil War an 1860 census showed 853 enslaved persons in St. Ferdinand Township among a total population of 4,800. Jesuit College, with 28 enslaved laborers to work the school's farms, became the area's biggest slaveholder. While no Carricos appear on the 1860 census as owning slaves, some relatives are listed, including Reuben Musick, Vincent's son-in-law. Reuben owned between 12 and 15.[12]

Prior to the Civil War, Missouri families became deeply divided over slavery. Reuben Carrico, one of Vincent's grandsons, signed an Oath of Allegiance to the Union, but testimony from a neighbor stated, "He expresses himself in every way that a man could against the U. S. Government and also Union men."[13] Reuben was fined and required to reaffirm his loyalty. Some of the Carricos' Patterson relatives by marriage were pro-slavery. But as early as 1819 a group of abolitionists met at Elisha Patterson's house (son of early settler John Patterson) to discuss admission of Missouri as a slave or free state. They adopted a resolution calling slavery contradictory to freedom and laws of nature and denounced it as a great evil. The group predicted this evil would bring hereditary misery on mankind, as well as the "judgment of a just, but angry God."[14] Though they lost their fight for Missouri's admission as a free state, the petition demonstrated substantial abolitionist sentiment in St. Ferdinand Township. On the opposite side of this issue, an enslaved family belonging to

William Patterson, Elisha's brother, escaped to Chicago but was returned to Patterson under a Fugitive Slave Act of 1850.[15] It required that slaves be returned to owners, even from a free state. It also made the federal government responsible for finding, returning and prosecuting escaped slaves. Positions on both sides galvanized after Dred Scott, an enslaved black man living in St. Louis, lost his ten-year battle for freedom. Scott had been taken by an owner out of Missouri to live in Illinois, a free state, and then to Wisconsin Territory, which outlawed slavery. After later returning to St. Louis, Scott argued that having lived in a free state and territory entitled him to freedom. Ultimately the U.S. Supreme Court ruled in 1857 that an enslaved man was not a citizen, and as another person's property, Scott had no standing to sue.

By the time Vincent died, many of his family and extended family resided in the Old Jamestown area. A town never actually existed there, though early land speculators hoped to build a settlement rivaling St. Louis. Instead, it remained a small farming community and became part of Florissant, with Old Jamestown Road and New Jamestown Road being the only significant references to earlier settlement efforts. Much of Carrico land was within an Old Jamestown area known as Possum Hollow. Unlike bluff terrain along the Missouri River that characterized much of Old Jamestown and Spanish Lake, Possum Hollow rested in a valley reaching down to the river. It had forests, swamps, fertile fields and land bordering on and replenished by the river. The

Notice of Vincent Carrico's death and burial in St. Ferdinand Catholic Church records. Transcribed by Dan and Marilyn Patterson Devaney: Vincent Cariko. On 26 March 1816, I, the undersigned priest, buried in the cemetery of this parish Vincent Carriko who died yesterday after having received all the sacraments of burial. He was buried in the presence of the undersigned witnesses, and a large crowd of people. Priest: M. Dumand; Witnesses: Asa Carrico [and others]. ("Early U.S. French Catholic Church Records (Drouin Collection), 1695-1954," Registers of St. Ferdinand de Florissant Catholic Church)

river became a mixed blessing, however, when flooding changed its course in the late 1800s. It gobbled up about 300 acres of Carrico farmland, leaving them with only a fraction of their inheritances. A historian, speaking about frightening sounds of large chunks of land falling into the Missouri River, wrote:

> *There is nothing so well calculated to disturb the slumbers of the owner of a farm thus encroached upon as this continual booming noise, admonishing him that the hungry river is banqueting on his land, and that it is being swallowed up, acre by acre, with no power to arrest the destruction.[16]*

Carricos took loss of their land in stride and bought other land in that area to grow wheat, corn and soybeans. Daniel's and Matilda's son, James "Walter" Carrico, established his home on what became Carrico Road, just down a hill from the intersection of Shackelford and Old Jamestown roads.

Walter's daughter, Margaret Ellen Carrico, and her husband, James Thompson of Scotland, also established a home and raised their children on Carrico Road. The road has twists, turns, overhanging tree branches and an aura of mystery. In 2012, *St. Louis Riverfront Times* published an article noting:

The old Carrico Family Cemetery sits on a bluff overlooking the Missouri River at a point where it empties into the Mississippi River.

On a windswept October evening, Carrico Road seems like the sort of place plucked right out of a Grimms' fairy tale. The winding stretch of asphalt disappears from one bend to the next. Fallen leaves swirl across the pavement, and at least eight signs along the shoulder of the roadway carry the same ominous message: 'No trespassing.'

This article goes on to say that the road has long been associated with an urban legend about a strange family of "hook men," ghosts with swollen heads, or mysterious hitchhikers from the great beyond lurking deep within the woods who sometimes "attack trespassers in a flurry of rage."[17]

Nature has threatened other areas in and around Old Jamestown, including a proliferation of sink holes characteristic of "karst" topography.* Formed in this case from limestone bluffs overlooking the river, holes develop when limestone dissolves, causing soil and everything above it to sink into a void.

A 1995 article in *Missouri Resources Magazine* pointed out that this area has hundreds of sink holes, ranging from a few feet to several feet in diameter, and from a few feet to more than 70 feet deep. The area has been declared nationally significant and extremely fragile in places, preventing much urban development that characterizes other parts of St. Louis County. [18]

It is unclear where early pioneers Vincent and Susannah are buried. A few descendants claim they are buried in the Carrico Family Cemetery, located on Vincent's original land. But legible remaining grave markers go back only to the 1850s. St. Ferdinand Church in

---

A terrain formed from dissolution of soluble rocks such as limestone, dolomite and gypsum.

A gathering of Carrico cousins at the home of Walter M. Carrico, Vincent's great great grandson. Aurelia Thompson Wehmer, daughter of Margaret Carrico and James Thompson, is at right in dark dress. James and Hazel Snoddy Wehmer later acquired this Carrico farmstead.

Florissant records interments for Vincent and Susannah in the old church graveyard. In 1900, however, the city decreed that all remains there be removed by families and reinterred in a new church cemetery or at a place of relatives' choosing. No records reflect where bodies were relocated, or whether they were moved, though rows of caskets have surfaced occasionally during flooding or construction. As part of city and county observances of the nation's bicentennial celebration in 1976, this property became Spanish Land Grant Park. A single marker at the park memorializes "the valiant pioneers" once buried there or who may still be there.[19] Valiant, indeed, the Carricos left their marks throughout the county.

Carrico Direct Line

Peter CARRICO Sr.
b: 1689 Normandy, France
d: 18 Oct 1765 Charles County, MD

Margaret GATES
b: Abt. 1715
m: Abt. 1738
d: Abt. 1767

James T. CARRICO Sr.
b: 1743 Charles County, MD
d: 11 Dec 1799 Charles County, MD

Elizabeth Catherine CLEMENTS
b: 1744 Charles County, MD
m: Abt. 1763 Charles County, MD
d: 05 Apr 1796 Charles County, MD

Vincent CARRICO
b: Bet. 1764–1765 Georgetown, MD
d: 26 Mar 1816 Spanish Lake, MO

Susannah QUICK
b: 18 Feb 1769 Cumberland, MD
m: 18 Feb 1796 Madison County, KY
d: 10 May 1830 St. Louis County, MO

David Daniel CARRICO
b: 01 Jan 1799 St. Louis County, MO
d: Bef. 14 May 1838 Florissant, MO

Matilda CARRICO
b: 1802 Kentucky
m: 25 Apr 1817 Nelson County, KY
d: 09 Aug 1820 St. Louis County, MO

James "Walter" CARRICO
b: 22 Jun 1818 Florissant, MO
d: 22 Aug 1868 Florissant, MO

Louesa DOWNS
b: 25 Sep 1823 Gettysburg, PA
m: 18 Nov 1841
d: 11 Oct 1863 Florissant, MO

Margaret Ellen CARRICO
b: 02 Jul 1849 Florissant, MO
d: 02 Mar 1922 Florissant, MO

James M. THOMPSON
b: 23 Dec 1843 Glasgow, Scotland
m: 19 Aug 1868 Florissant, MO
d: 22 Sep 1916 Florissant, MO

Aurelia Ethel THOMPSON
b: 30 Jul 1887 Florissant, MO
d: 04 Dec 1976 Florissant, MO

Louis (Ludwig) August WEHMER
b: 24 Oct 1886 Florissant, MO
m: 20 Mar 1913 Florissant, MO
d: 18 Aug 1952 Florissant, MO

James Henry WEHMER
b: 26 Mar 1919 Florissant, MO
d: 10 Sep 1978 Florissant, MO

End Notes

[1] William L. Thomas, *History of St. Louis County, Missouri,* vol. I (St. Louis: S. J. Clarke Publishing Co., 1911, 20.

[2] Perry S. Rader, *History of Missouri: from the Earliest Times to the Present,* revised (Jefferson City, MO: Hugh Stephens Printing Co., 1907), 372.

[3] "Fort Belle Fontaine, Missouri – The First Fort of the West," (LegendsofAmerica.com).

[4] Douglas Walter Bond, *The Spanish Domination of Upper Louisiana* (Madison: State Historical Society of Wisconsin, 1914), 87.

[5] David T. Bunch, "A History of the Salem Baptist Church" 1957, 3-6; Ralph E. Wehmer, "Salem Baptist Church History, 1997, 1-2,; documents located at Salem Baptist Church, Shackelford Road at Old Jamestown Road.

[6] Walter Robinson Smith, *Brief History of the Louisiana Territory* (St. Louis: The St. Louis News Company, 1904), 52-23.

[7] Arkansas Commissioner of State Lands, "Spanish Land Grants," *Historical Documents, Maps & More* (history.cosl.org).

[8] Peggy Cruse, *Old Jamestown Across the Ages: Highlights and Stories of Old Jamestown, Missouri* (Florissant: Peace Weavers, LLC, 2018) 67-70; 72-73.

[9] Vincent Carrico land grants, 19 Oct 1802, Charles County (Land Records) Deed, Liber IB 5, folio 265-281, MSA CE82-43, Acc. no. CR 42,843-1, Maryland State Archives, Annapolis, MD (mdlandrec.net).

[10] Vincent Carrico will, 16 Mar 1816, *St. Louis Probate Records 1804-1849,* "Record of Deeds," vol. R, 444-447, Missouri State Archives, Jefferson City, MO.

[11] Andrew J. Theising, ed., *In the Walnut Grove: a Consideration of the People Enslaved In and Around Florissant, Missouri* (Florissant: Florissant Valley Historical Society, 2020), 9.

[12] Cindy Winkler, compiler, "1860 Census, St. Ferdinand Township, Enslaved Inhabitants by Slaveholder Household," *In the Walnut Grove,* 44-47.

[13] Winkler, "Slavery in North County," *In the Walnut Grove,* 114.

[14] Theising, *In the Walnut Grove,* 148-151. Reprinted from *Missouri Gazette and Public Advertiser,* 23 Jun 1819, 3.

[15] Ibid., 152.

[16] Philip E. Chappell, "Floods in the Missouri River," *Kansas State Historical Society,* vol. X, George W. Martin, ed. (Topeka, Kan.: State Printing Office, 1908).

[17] Leah Greenbaum, "Five St. Louis Ghost Stories That Just Won't Die," *Riverfront Times,* 25 Oct 2012 (riverfronttimes.com).

[18] James Vandike, "Living with the Sinks," *Missouri Resources Magazine* (Division of Geology and Land Survey, Missouri Department of Natural Resources), 1995. From 1988 field trip report reprinted in Peggy Kruse, *Old Jamestown Across the Ages,* 168-170.

[19] "Florissant's First Cemetery," *Historic Florissant, Inc.,* Florissant, Missouri, 21 Oct 2020 (historicflorissant.com).

This postcard reproduces a painting by Sam Bough showing the Glasgow Bridge in 1850, around the time the Thomsons left for America. View is from the Gorbals side, looking across the River Clyde. (Mitchell Library, Glasgow Collection Postcards, Glasgow City Council, Libraries Information and Learning)

Scotland in his Blood
James Thompson

James Thompson entered this world amid belching smoke and acrid air from cotton mills enveloping his family's tenement house in Glasgow, Scotland. It is remarkable that he would depart this world 72 years later and 4,000 miles away amid fresh air and the pleasant smell of newly mown hay on his farm in St. Louis County, Missouri.

At the time James was born, just before Christmas in 1843, Glasgow and districts on its east side already had fallen victim to industrialization's negative consequences. They included noxious gases rising from factories, dangerous industrial waste, overcrowding, lack of worker housing, contagious diseases and raw sewage dumped into River Clyde. Glasgow grew from fifth largest city in Great Britain in 1801 to the second largest (exceeded only by London) in just 30 years, from 77,385 to 202,426 people.[1]

By the time James's parents, Robert Thomson (later Americanized to Thompson) and Margaret (Maggie) McLean, married in 1837[2] at least 134 cotton mills had located in and around Glasgow. As the city expanded, cotton topped tobacco as a source of wealth, making mill owners rich, but requiring a large labor force to process raw cotton being shipped from the United States and elsewhere. People crammed into tenement houses near factories where they worked, sometimes with six people or more living in one room.[3] Margaret's family resided in tenements in the Calton district of Barony Parish; Robert's family lived in similar circumstances in the Tradeston district of Gorbals Parish. Facing each other across River Clyde, these two industrial areas were connected by a bridge with a toll bar that further exploited people traveling back and forth between homes and factories.

Workers were taken advantage of even in death, often being buried in common grounds of overcrowded graveyards with no markers. Adding to such indignities, during the early 1800s Glasgow experienced a shortage of cadavers at its medical school. When people died of mysterious illnesses, medical students occasionally attempted to dig up their bodies for study. The River Clyde toll keeper on the

Gorbals side had a keen eye for recognizing and stopping such unscrupulous characters. A story is told, however, that on one occasion two university students exhumed a body from a Gorbals grave late at night, dressed it appropriately and propped it between them in their carriage. As they approached the bridge, one paid the toll, while the other held the head of their "companion," telling him they would be having breakfast soon. The tollkeeper shined his lantern on the supposedly sick passenger and exclaimed, "Oh, puir auld bodie, he looks unco [strangely] ill; drive cannily home, lads, drive cannily."[4]

Life wasn't always harsh for the McLeans and Thomsons. When Maggie's grandparents lived in Calton before the 19th century, it remained a rural area known for handloom weavers who worked out of their homes and sold their cloth in Glasgow. As the need for woven cloth grew, outside competition did not sit well with the Glasgow Weavers' Guild. This resulted in taxes imposed on goods coming in, along with constant bickering among Calton weavers, Glasgow weavers and merchants. Animosities exploded into what became known as the Calton Weavers Strike of 1787. Three weavers were killed outright, three mortally wounded and others injured by police trying to break up rioting. Historians consider this the earliest major industrial dispute in Scottish history, and Calton weavers became Scotland's first working-class martyrs.[5]

As the world's voracious appetite for cotton consumed this area, developers razed bucolic weavers' cottages to make way for factories and tenements. Barony and Gorbals parishes became part of Glasgow proper. Along with displaced families in both parishes, Scottish migrants poured in from the highlands due to a Highlands Clearance Act, which evicted farm tenants to make way for large-scale sheep farming. Immigrants also came from Ireland where drought meant people could no longer feed starving families.

Alexander McLean (Maggie's father and James's maternal grandfather) was a weaver transitioning from hand looms to automated mills. He married Mary McCallum in 1811 in Barony Parish, and Maggie arrived in 1813 as the first of their nine children who survived to adulthood.[6] Not long after birth of their last child in 1832, Alexander died of unknown causes.

By the 1841 census, his widow Mary and six of their children lived in a Calton tenement district at the intersection of Bell Street and Mill Road.[7] Four cotton mills operated within a three-block radius of their home. McLean children still at home without a main breadwinner had to work in mills or find suitable employment elsewhere to make ends meet. The oldest son labored as a mechanic, while another took up lithography.* Even

_____

* *A printing method using simple chemical processes.*

Textile mills were dangerous places for children. Above, a barefoot boy works on a piece of machinery. Below, a young girl has to stand on a box to perform her assigned task.
(Library of Congress, Lewis Wickes Hines)

younger children took dangerous jobs in mills; owners hired small nimble workers who could move quickly around and under machinery. One of the McLean children was a carder, operating a machine to straighten and align cotton fibers. Two children worked as piecers, which required young children to walk along moving machinery to piece together loose threads. Though no occupation is listed in the 1841 census for the youngest child, she may have worked as an unpaid scavenger, a job reserved for smaller children who crawled beneath machinery to clean up oil, dust and dirt.[8]

Before child labor laws took effect, Scotland was known for child injuries via machinery.[9] Some had skin scraped off knuckles to the bone; others had finger crushed, or a joint snipped off by spinning cogs. After being patched up by a surgeon, injured children sometimes returned to the factory floor. A memoir published by a former piecer in 1841, *A Narrative of the Experience and Sufferings of William Dodd a Factory Cripple*, remembers young co-workers who died or had limbs severed after being caught in a machine. Dodd points out other causes of child injury, including his own crippling from long hours in stationery positions since age 5, before bones had fully matured. These misshapen bones caused poor circulation, ultimately requiring amputation of his right arm from below the elbow. He recalls, "A great many were made cripples by over-exertion. Among those who have been brought up from infancy with me in the factories, and whom death has spared, few have escaped without some injury."[10]

To escape dismal living conditions and avoid treacherous working conditions for their children, Maggie's sister Mary and her husband, Charles Hamilton, immigrated to St. Louis by way of New Orleans in 1842. Six younger siblings and their mother, Mary, followed in 1845.[11] When Maggie's husband died of a fever in 1847 while in his 30s, she determined to immigrate to St. Louis as well. While mills and poor working conditions also existed in American cities, Scottish emigrants perceived greater opportunities for improving their living and working conditions. Maggie knew that if she and her children stayed, things would only get worse -- and indeed they did for others. An 1863 report by the city's medical officer described the area of Glasgow where Thomsons and McLeans had lived 15 years earlier as "not surpassed by any close in the city for filth, misery, crime and disease... inhabited by a most wretched class of individuals."[12]

In February 1848 the merchant barque *St. Mary's* arrived in Glasgow with a cargo of cotton from Mobile, Alabama, to feed the region's hungry mills. The captain advertised that he would make an immediate return trip, this time to New Orleans for more cotton, and was accepting applications for freight and passengers. As soon as Maggie read this news she rushed to a shipping agent and booked passage for herself and her four children – Margaret, Gilbert, James and Alexander.[13] They sailed on March 4, 1848, reaching New Orleans a few weeks later, then traveling by steamboat up the Mississippi to St. Louis,

A 19th century merchant vessel carries immigrants amid cargo. Ships regularly sailed to southern ports, then made their return to Glasgow, Liverpool, Bristol and London ports with loads of cotton for British textile mills. (Copy of 1850 English wood engraving, Granger)

where other family members had located. At that time only New York surpassed the Port of New Orleans in number of international arrivals, given its easy route to the country's interior. Immigrants could disembark at many ports along the Mississippi as well as its major tributaries, including the Missouri and Ohio rivers.[14]

When the Thomsons stepped onto a cobblestone levee in St. Louis, they entered a burgeoning city. From 17,000 in 1840, its population grew to 160,000 over the next 20 years, due in large part to immigrant families such as the Thomsons.[15] At times as many as

170 steamboats lined up three deep along a 15-mile riverfront. Difficulties in accommodating rapid growth, however, meant the Thomsons' struggles continued when they reached St. Louis. Conditions there were almost as bad as those in Scotland. Less than a year after their arrival, the St. Louis Cholera Epidemic of 1849 wiped out nearly 10 percent of the city's population, due to unsanitary conditions. Neither docked steamboats nor the city had sewer systems. This combination proved deadly, with an official death toll from cholera within the city proper reaching 4,317 during the epidemic.[16] Many residents suspected that Chouteau's Pond, a large manmade lake in the

This wood engraving shows a line of steamboats moored on the levee at St. Louis about the time the Thompsons arrived. (Harper's Weekly, Photographed by R. Benecke.)

Cholera warnings were posted throughout the St. Louis area in 1949

city, played a major role in spreading this disease. The pond began as a favorite place for picnics. But as the city and its industries grew, businesses such as tanneries and butcher shops crowded its banks, quickly turning it into a cesspool. One story appearing in a Belleville, Illinois, newspaper on July 12, 1849, reported that trash and industrial waste weren't the only things found when they drained the pond in an effort to stop contagion:

SHOCKING: We are informed by one of the police, last evening, that seven coffins, each containing a dead body, were taken from Chouteau's pond yesterday. Pieces of iron were tied to each coffin, and they were sunk a short distance from the shore, opposite Mr. Blow's lead factory. We presume they were the remains of persons who had died of cholera in the district known as "Shepard's Grave Yard."[17]

An article about James Thompson in later years indicates that his mother died shortly after their arrival and was buried in Belleville, across the river from St. Louis. It is possible that Maggie fell victim to this epidemic, and her daughter Margaret may have succumbed as well. No record of either death has been found, possibly due to mass graves being used for cholera victims.[18] After Maggie's death her orphaned children were shuffled among relatives and friends. Gilbert and Alexander moved to Memphis with their uncle Gilbert McLean and his family.[19] James, however, remained in St. Louis and was taken in by Stokes Thorpe, a dealer in hides and furs who also had a farm in St. Louis County. James

stayed with the Thorpe family while attaining an education. He then departed at age 15 to live with his uncle Matthew McLean in Stillwater, Minnesota.[20] James trained as a mechanic, but found it too monotonous. After two years James returned to St. Louis and worked as a lithographer for an uncle still in St. Louis, Alexander McLean. James didn't work at an office job for long. Wanting to experience wide-open spaces, he moved in with the family of a young farmer in St. Louis County, George Bent.[21] James found his calling there, including putting his mechanical skills to good use in learning to operate a threshing machine. High demand for wheat threshing services throughout his life made him well known to St.

Threshing wheat in St. Louis County. Invention of mechanized machines in the 19th century revolutionized the process of separating grain from stalk and husk.

James Thompson and Margaret Ellen Carrico Thompson home on Carrico Road.
All their children were raised in this house.

Louis County farmers. But one day he experienced a threat to his feeling of independence and freedom. While threshing in a field during the Civil War, officers of the Missouri Militia arrested him, suspecting James of being a southern sympathizer. They threw him into a Union prison, most likely Gratiot Street Prison in downtown St. Louis. It held citizens who supported the Rebel cause, as well as captured Confederate soldiers. After several months in prison, authorities released

him when no evidence could be found of collusion with enemy forces.

In 1868 James married Margaret Ellen Carrico,[22] from one of the oldest families in St. Louis County, as well as being immigrants to America before the Revolutionary War. Her family did not look favorably on this marriage since Thompson was both an immigrant and a field hand. Nevertheless, the marriage proceeded, and Carricos quickly changed their

James Thompson
in his later years

Margaret Ellen Carrico
Thompson around
time of her marriage

James Thompson family on the porch of their house.

minds about this hard-working Scotsman. When Margaret's father died just a few days after her marriage, she inherited 47 acres of land. This became the nucleus of a Thompson family homestead where they raised three sons and six daughters,* including Aurelia who later married Louis Wehmer.

James added another 60 acres to this original property, but he experienced a setback when the Missouri River changed its course and swallowed up 70 acres of his fertile bottom land. Being accustomed to hardships, he took this hurdle in stride and became a successful and widely respected farmer and custom thresher in the area for 50 years. A community servant in all things, James served on the local school board for 40 years and became known throughout the county as being highly principled and community minded.

Though he left many hard times in Scotland behind him, James remained loyal to the country of his birth and took great pride in being called a "Scotsman." When he died in 1916, his tombstone proudly proclaimed, "James Thompson, born in Glasgow, Scotland."

---

*They had 10 children but their first son died just a few months after birth.

James and Margaret Ellen Carrico Thompson memorial marker at Cold Water Cemetery.
Tombstone gives his death date as Sept. 21, 1916, though his death certificate says Sept. 22, 1916.

Thompson Direct Line

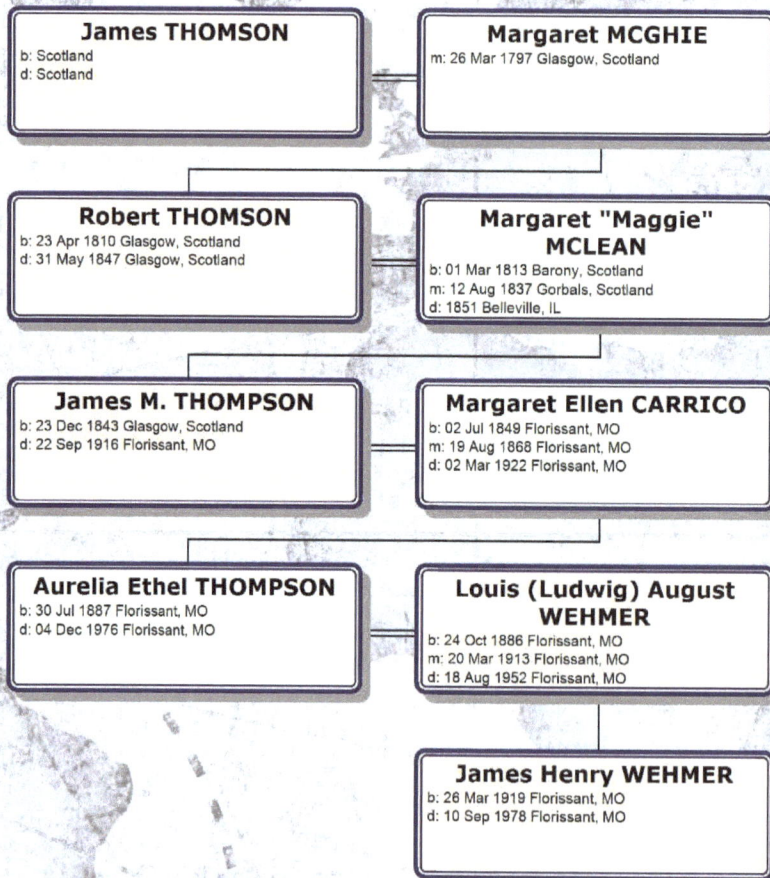

James THOMSON
b: Scotland
d: Scotland

Margaret MCGHIE
m: 26 Mar 1797 Glasgow, Scotland

Robert THOMSON
b: 23 Apr 1810 Glasgow, Scotland
d: 31 May 1847 Glasgow, Scotland

Margaret "Maggie" MCLEAN
b: 01 Mar 1813 Barony, Scotland
m: 12 Aug 1837 Gorbals, Scotland
d: 1851 Belleville, IL

James M. THOMPSON
b: 23 Dec 1843 Glasgow, Scotland
d: 22 Sep 1916 Florissant, MO

Margaret Ellen CARRICO
b: 02 Jul 1849 Florissant, MO
m: 19 Aug 1868 Florissant, MO
d: 02 Mar 1922 Florissant, MO

Aurelia Ethel THOMPSON
b: 30 Jul 1887 Florissant, MO
d: 04 Dec 1976 Florissant, MO

Louis (Ludwig) August WEHMER
b: 24 Oct 1886 Florissant, MO
m: 20 Mar 1913 Florissant, MO
d: 18 Aug 1952 Florissant, MO

James Henry WEHMER
b: 26 Mar 1919 Florissant, MO
d: 10 Sep 1978 Florissant, MO

End Notes

[1] Ian Mortimor, *The Time Traveler's Guide to Regency Britain* (New York: Pegasus Books, Ltd., 2022), 18.

[2] Robert Thomson and Margaret McLean marriage record, 12 Aug 1837, "Church Records," Gorbals Parish, Scotland, National Records of Scotland (nrscotland.gov.uk).

[3] David William, "Glasgow: History-Early Nineteenth Century," *The Glasgow Guide* (Edinburgh: Birlinn Books, 1998; scotland-guide.co.uk).

[4] John Ord, *The Story of the Barony of Gorbals* (Paisley: Alexander Gardner, 1919), 37-38.

[5] Christina O'Neill, "The Calton Weavers, the 1820 Radical War and Scotland's first working-class martyrs" (glasgowlive.co.uk).

[6] Alexander McLean-Mary McCallum marriage, 8 Dec 1811, Old Parish Records, Barony Parish, Scotlands People (scotlandspeople.gov.uk); Minnie H. Roever, McLean Family Record, sent to her father, Alexander Hamilton, by a cousin, Peter M. Hansen, 30 Jan 1895.

[7] 1841 Scotland Census, Mary McLean household, Barony, Middle Calton, Lanarkshire, Scotland, National Records of Scotland, Scotland's People (scotlandspeople.gov.uk).

[8] Thomas Mulrooney, "The Ultimate Guide To Cotton Fabric Manufacturing: Part 2 - Carding & Combing The Cotton," *Vision Linens Blog*, 4 Dec 2020 (visionlinens.com/blog).

[9] Joseph Vera, et al, "Child Labor in the Cotton Mill," *The Industrial Revolution and Colonialism: An Educational Website*, Humanities 10, (tirac.weebly.com).

[10] William Dodd, *A Narrative of the Experience and Sufferings of William Dodd a Factory Cripple* (London: L. & G. Seeley, 1841), 16.

[11] Hamilton family immigration, *Passenger Lists of Vessels Arriving At New Orleans, Louisiana, 1820-1902*, 13 May 1843, *Claiborne*, Liverpool to New Orleans (Ancestry.com); Mary McLean family immigration, *New Orleans, Passenger List Quarterly Abstracts, 1820-1875*, 10 Mar 1845, *Palmyra*, Liverpool to New Orleans (Ancestry.com).

[12] "Glasgow Stuff. Glasgow from the Past. Old and New Street Names" (urbanglasgow.co.uk).

[13] *Glasgow Herald*, Glasgow, Scotland: 18 Feb 1848 ("Ship News" and "At Glasgow-For New Orleans") and 10 Mar 1848 ("From the Clyde Bill of Entry, Arrivals and Imports. Sailed" (Newspapers.com); Margaret Thomson family immigration, *Passenger Lists of Vessels Arriving At New Orleans, Louisiana, 1820-1902*, 1 May 1848, *St. Mary's*, Glasgow to New Orleans (Ancestry.com).

[14] "Genealogy: Port of New Orleans has Unique History" 25 Jun 2017, *Tribune-Star* e-paper (tribstar.com).

[15] "St. Louis: Becoming a City (1850-1900," *Gateway Arch National Park Website* (nps.gov).

[16] Elizabeth Davis, "Historically Yours: St. Louis Cholera Epidemic of 1849," *News Tribune*, Jefferson City, MO, 23 Jul 2019 (newstribune.com).

[17] "Shocking," *The Semi-Weekly Advocate*, 12 July 1849, 2. (Newspapers.com.)

[18] William L. Thomas, "James Thompson Biography," *History of St. Louis County, Missouri* (St. Louis: S. J. Clarke Publishing Co., 1911) 303-304.

[19] 1860 U. S. Federal Census, Gilbert McLean household, Memphis, Shelby County, TN.

[20] 1857 Minnesota Territorial Census, Matthew McClain household, Stillwater, Washington County, Minnesota Territory.

[21] 1860 U. S. Federal Census, James M. Thompson in George Bent household, St Louis County, MO.

Eickhorst Windmill in Hille
community. The mill was acquired by
miller Karl Heinrich Storck in 1842
and operated by the family until 1968.
It was restored in the late 1970s.
(Christian Kortum, Flickr)

A Long Way from Prussia

Heinrich (Henry) Wehmer
And Louise Buhrmester

Compared to other family lines, Wehmers and Buhrmesters became relative newcomers to the United States. Though they arrived separately in 1867, both families emigrated from Hille in Prussia. Heinrich August Eduard Wehmer came with a friend, while Sophie Marie Louise Buhrmester, who later became his wife, arrived with her parents and siblings.

Though Prussia no longer exists, Hille remains a largely agricultural community in the Minden-Lubbecke district of North Rhine-Westphalia, one of Germany's 16 states. Its fertile lands are nestled between Minden Forest to the Northeast, Weser River to the East and The Great Peat Bog, formed during the Ice Age, lying to the South. This varied terrain is characterized by scattered farms bordered by copses and hedges. Along with traditional farmsteads, a few early structures remain, including a former rye distillery that processed Hiller Moorbrand, a schnaps-based liquor. Five Dutch-type windmills only work to varying degrees today, but they provide a glimpse into an early milling process for grain.

An open market has been held biannually in Hille in April and September since 1564 and continues to bring its community together. Hille's village church dates from 1523. It was Catholic for a brief time before becoming Evangelical Lutheran during a 16th century Reformation. Tombstones from its old cemetery surround the church. Generations of Wehmers and Buhrmesters were baptized and married in this church; most likely some faded tombstones once bore their names. Baptized in this church in 1852, Henry was the son of Johann Carl Heinrich Wehmer and Caroline Marie Louise Niermeier, whose families farmed in this region for centuries.

Hille during 19ᵗʰ century Prussia was a region of farms and windmills. Entire families labored in the fields, such as these German workers above.

According to family tradition, the name "Wehmer" is an old term for "farmer" in a Low German dialect known as Hiller Pratt, once spoken almost exclusively around Hille.[1] In early Wehmer family records the phrase "Colon Riepen" occasionally appears. Colon comes from the Latin word "colonus," which in early Roman times meant a free farmer who settled in newly conquered territories. As found in German records, it typically referred to an independent farmer with inheritable rights to a piece of land, but who did not have outright ownership. A lease could be passed down to widows and children, with family remaining on the land so long as a legitimate

heir existed. The second name in this phrase, "Riepen" in the case of Wehmer records, refers to an original owner of the land. The land's name never changed, even if purchased or inherited by someone outside an original family. New owners often changed or added the farm name to their surname. Even when a daughter inherited ownership, her new husband usually changed his name to hers to keep a farm name intact.[2] It appears that Wehmers for many generations farmed land owned by a Riepen family or later owners who took the surname Riepen.

Henry's mother died when he was six years old, shortly after birth of her fifth child in 1858.[3] Henry went to live with Henry Niemeyer's* family, possibly his mother's brother or another Niermeier relative.[4] This family apparently took charge of getting Henry, and perhaps his siblings, through school while their widower father worked. Schooling was mandatory from ages 5 to 13 or 14 (at least eight years) thanks to Prussia's strong focus on education.

King Frederick William I enacted laws in 1717 proclaiming compulsory basic education for both boys and girls. He demanded that his subjects be able to read, write and do basic math, though he met public resistance at the time. Many parents considered it an intrusion on their privacy and prerogatives as parents.[5] His successor, Frederick II, significantly expanded Prussia's school system, requiring that all young citizens not only learn basics, but become people capable of reasoning and learning for themselves. His 1763 education reforms made Prussia one of the world's first countries to introduce tax-funded and compulsory primary education with a standardized state curriculum and national exams. By comparison, England and France did not enact successful compulsory education until the 1880s.[6] Elements of Prussia's system became educational models for other countries, including the United States. Frederick II's reforms went beyond education to include sweeping changes that transformed

Prussia into a modern state, earning for him the nickname "Frederick the Great" from countrymen and historians.

When Henry reached 14 and was completing this mandatory education his father died, and the following year he and his friend Charley Gerling, probably a cousin,** left their homeland in search of a new life in America.[7] His schoolmate Louise and her family emigrated that year as well. Political and economic unrest in Germany led to an exodus for many. Prussia had become a dominant power among 39 Germanic states created after defeat of Napoleon in 1815, and the 1866 Austro-Prussian War consolidated its power. By 1867, armies of almost all Germanic states had merged into a powerful Prussian Army, leading the way for creation of a German Empire in 1871.

From its establishment as an empire in 1701, Prussia became fanatical in achieving military prowess. King Frederick I realized that security depended on strength of a Prussian Army, and his military force grew to about 40,000 soldiers by end of his reign in 1713.[8] King Frederick's son and successor, King Frederick William, took his military preoccupation to extremes, continually marching and drilling soldiers and subjecting them to austere conditions. By the end of his reign in 1740, he had doubled the army's size to 90,000, making it fourth largest in Europe, despite Prussia ranking twelfth in population.[9] Strength of this army led French

---

Niemeyer may be misspelled in the record source, or a variation on the name Niermeier.
**Heinrich Wehmer's mother and Charley Gerling's mother both were Niermeiers before marriage.*

wit, writer and philosopher Voltaire to remark, "Where some states have an army, the Prussian Army has a state." [10]

One of Frederick William's oddest preoccupations included an experimental regiment of "giants," nicknamed the Long Lads or Potsdam Giants, composed of men at least 6 feet, 2 inches tall. At that time such height was rare, so recruiting 3,000 men required a "manhunt" across Europe. He also sought tall women who could be induced to marry these soldiers in hopes of producing even taller offspring. These recruits received higher salaries and benefits than other soldiers. Most proved unfit for actual military duty due to their size, but the king marched them up and down a royal courtyard constantly for his pleasure. They basically served as decoration, used for parades and impressing foreign dignitaries. [11]

In many cases, young men nearing draft age emigrated after the Austro-Prussian War in 1866 to avoid mandatory military duty in Prussia's army, given the prospect of additional conflicts on Europe's horizon. A list of "secret emigration" from the Administrative District of Minden shows Henry among those who departed in 1867, but he is included in an addendum. This section of the document identified emigrants who would have appeared on conscription lists in the near future. [12]

Christian Buhrmester and his family traveled aboard the S. S. Weser, *shown here making its maiden voyage between Bremen and New York on June 1, 1867.*

Amid political turmoil as Prussia flexed its military muscle during the 1860s, areas around Hille suffered from crop failures, high prices for farm inputs and unemployment. Land redistribution resulting from territorial wars and conflicts led to many small farmers being without land or the possibility of acquiring land. More than half of Prussian emigrants in the mid to late 1800s were farmers such as Christian Wilhelm Buhrmester and his family. He and his wife Caroline departed Bremen on June 1, 1867, with six children and another one on the way.

The Buhrmesters traveled aboard *S. S. Weser* making its maiden voyage and sailed with the western winds to arrive in New York 16 days later. The 365-foot ocean liner accommodated 60 passengers in first class, 120 in second class, and 700 in steerage.[13] The Buhrmesters likely traveled in steerage, which had the cheapest accommodations. Transatlantic voyages in the 19th century were difficult for all. But for a woman six months pregnant with six other children in tow, it became almost intolerable. Pitching and rolling vessels caused seasickness. Climbing up and down steep ladders between decks was an ordeal, if not impossible.[14] Once they arrived in New York and got their land legs back, the Buhrmesters probably remained in the East until birth of their seventh child, three months after reaching America. They then moved to Nashville in Washington County, Illinois, across the Mississippi River from St. Louis.

The St. Louis area had become a popular destination for Germans. A first sizable wave swept in during the 1830s and increased

Caroline Schlinger Buhrmester sailed for America while six months into her seventh pregnancy.

steadily until the Civil War. Some known as "Forty-Eighters," who participated in or supported the Revolutions of 1848,[15] favored unification of Germany, a more democratic government and guarantees of human rights. When these efforts at reform did not materialize, many made their way to America and elsewhere. This diverse group included professionals, merchants, artisans, farmers and others. Many continued their occupations in their adopted country and contributed significantly to a burgeoning St. Louis. From 1830 to 1850, the city's population grew from 4,977 to 77,860, with rankings increasing from 57th to 8th largest city in the country.[16]

One of the most well-known German immigrants to St. Louis, Eberhard Anheuser, arrived in 1843 and became owner of a large soap and candle company in the city. Though he had no brewing experience, in 1860

Henry and Louise used a German song book, shown with cover and title page, to record family information and connect with their culture. (Norman Wehmer)

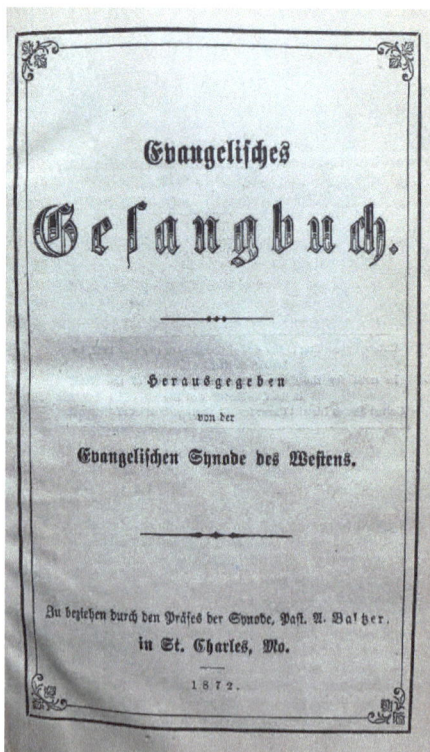

Anheuser acquired the failing neighborhood Bavarian Brewery, established several years earlier by German brewers who brought their trade with them. Four years later his son-in-law, Adolphus Busch, joined him, and they built Anheuser-Busch Brewing Association into one of the world's leading breweries.[17] Busch, who emigrated from Germany in 1857, served in the Union Army during America's Civil War prior to partnering with his father-in-law. Like Busch, many German immigrants coming to St. Louis at that time became ardent abolitionists. Some became disillusioned on arrival by Missouri's slavery laws and went back across the Mississippi River to St. Clair and Washington counties in the free state of Illinois.[18] Many others remained in St. Louis, however, and quickly became outspoken critics of slavery. Germans came to America for freedom, and they resented both slavery and the political power it gave slaveholders.

German immigrants helped prevent Missouri from seceding from the Union, even though it remained a slave state. When Missouri governor Claiborne Jackson, a secessionist, could not convince a majority in the state legislature to desert the Union, he decided to take control of the state by force. To do that required using his Missouri Militia to seize the federal arsenal in St. Louis. German organizations within the city began preparations to assist in defending the arsenal against this attack, including training volunteers, securing weapons and coordinating activities against the governor. More than 5,000 men immediately enlisted in the 3rd Missouri Volunteers. Of the first 4,200 men,

4,100 were German.[19] Faced with this larger force on the day of their planned attack, Confederates surrendered without a fight, and Missouri remained in the Union.

Once the war ended, a new wave of Germans immigrated to St. Louis and counties in Illinois. They chose this region based on rosy reports and romantic propaganda from earlier immigrants. These later immigrants farmed land around St. Louis amid rolling hills, vast prairies, climate similar to home and fertile soil deposited from the Missouri and Mississippi rivers. Many lived in already-established German communities to maintain their culture. By 1870, Germans comprised more than half of Washington County, Illinois, residents, with so many from the Minden district that one town took the name "New Minden." Across the river in St. Louis, one in four persons in 1880 claimed to belong to an ethnic group, with slightly more than half being Germans. About 46 percent of public school children were German, and many continued to receive lessons in German.[20]

The Buhrmester family ultimately settled in Hoyleton, a farming precinct in Washington County with a population nearly 100 percent German. Like other German communities in the county, Hoyleton took on many "old country" characteristics. Houses built close to streets had space in the rear for a garden, chicken house, smokehouse and barn. German housewives canned and preserved fruits and vegetables during summers. They ground wheat and corn into flour at a mill, and crocks of sauerkraut filled cellars. Farmers slaughtered and smoked meat, mostly pork,

Heinrich August Eduard Wehmer

and traded produce at a village store for other essentials. Wood cut from their property heated homes.[21]

The 1870 census shows that Henry had a grocery store job in the heart of St. Louis,[22] but he apparently missed his agricultural lifestyle in Germany. In less than a year he made his way to St. Louis County and worked as a farm hand for about eight years. Once he had some money in his pocket, Henry went to Illinois where the Buhrmesters had settled. He made Louise his bride in 1876, a year after her father died, and they moved to St. Louis County. Henry farmed there – a tradition that passed down through the next two generations.

Louise and her children moved to this house in 1904. It remained in the Wehmer family nearly 80 years.

Death of Louise's dad at age 49 left his widow, Caroline, to care for their children, including an eighth child just two years old.[23] Fortunately older children helped tend to younger ones. German naming patterns make it particularly difficult to follow Buhrmester and Wehmer family members. In Germany, each child received a name for everyday use, called its "Rufname," and this name typically came second or third in a sequence of given names. First names often meant nothing, and it was common for all boys or all girls in a family to have the same names appearing somewhere in their sequence. Often the name used was underlined to avoid confusion.[24] In Louise's case, all three of her sisters shared at least one

name with her, and both of Henry's brothers shared at least one.*

Henry and Louise ultimately had nine children, including two adopted sons, and all had similar name combinations. As German Lutherans, they started out attending Salem Evangelical Lutheran Church in Black Jack, Missouri, about eight miles from home. They christened their first child there.[25] They also purchased burial plots, beginning a tradition of Wehmer burials in the Lutheran cemetery. Sunday trips could be arduous, however, and soon they became members of Salem Baptist Church near a farm that Henry rented. By the 1860s, increasing German immigrants in this

---

* *Buhrmester Siblings: Caroline <u>Marie</u> Louise, Sophie Marie <u>Louise</u> (married Heinrich Wehmer), <u>Caroline</u> Wilhelmine Louise, Caroline Wilhelmine <u>Sophie</u>, <u>Christian</u> Henry, <u>Frederich</u> William, Henry <u>Louis</u>, and <u>Henry</u> August. Wehmer Siblings: <u>Marie</u> Louise, <u>Heinrich</u> August Edward (married Louise Buhrmester), <u>Christian</u> Heinrich August, <u>Caroline</u> Marie Louise, and Carl <u>Friedrich</u> August.*

church resulted in a minister being brought in once a month to deliver a sermon in German.[26] Henry became an active member of the church, including serving on its finance committee and as Sunday School leader.

After an untimely death in 1900 at age 48, his widow Louise managed their farm with help from her sons. In 1903 she purchased 40 acres of adjacent land and moved her family in 1904 into what became the family home on Douglas Road. Upon Louise's death, her unmarried son Paul lived in the house until his death in 1978. Though he willed their family homestead to the church, it ultimately fell into private hands.[27] Many Salem Baptist Church members were buried in the old Cold Water Church cemetery. Henry and Louise, however, were buried in Salem Lutheran Church's cemetery, where they had first been members. Eight of their nine children are interred there as well, along with other relatives.

From a lone boy coming from Prussia just after America's Civil War, the Wehmer family line exploded. Henry and Louise had nine children, 11 grandchildren, 30 great grandchildren, and numerous second and third great grandchildren. The farming tradition and large families working their land are reflected in generations that followed.

What became Brown School, pictured above in the late 1800s, played a major role in the lives of Wehmer children. Henry's and Louise's children are among those pictured but are not identified. Later it became a parsonage for Salem Baptist Church.

Louise Buhrmester Wehmer with her children and a few neighbors, ca. 1913. Back row from left, Esther Wehmer, Aurelia (Rill) Thompson Wehmer, Louis Wehmer, Genevieve Buhrmester, George Mullandy, Annie Ahlers, Joe Teason. Middle row, Ed Wehmer, Carrie Wehmer, Louise Buhrmester Wehmer, Mrs. Mullandy. Front row, Paul Wehmer, Loy Teason, Fred Wehmer holding Emily Wehmer, Helen Grueninger, Henry Wehmer.

Wehmer Direct Line

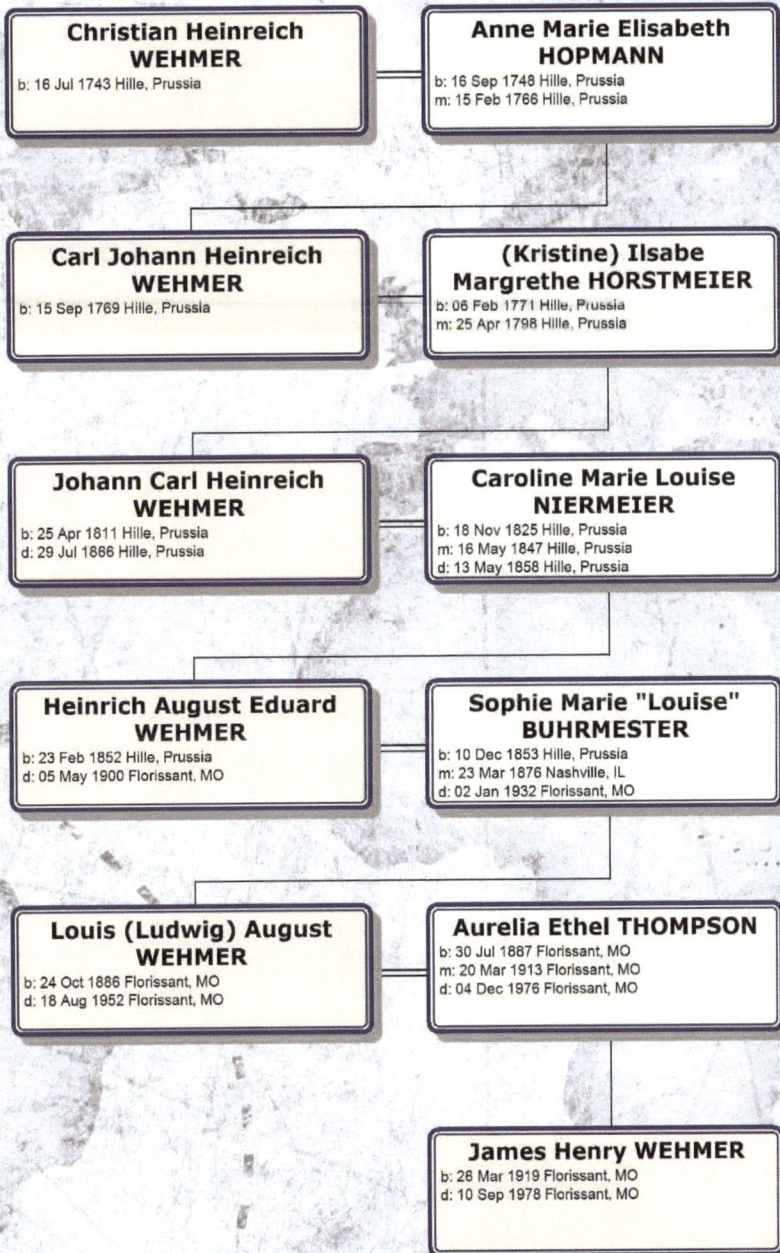

Christian Heinreich WEHMER
b: 16 Jul 1743 Hille, Prussia

Anne Marie Elisabeth HOPMANN
b: 16 Sep 1748 Hille, Prussia
m: 15 Feb 1766 Hille, Prussia

Carl Johann Heinreich WEHMER
b: 15 Sep 1769 Hille, Prussia

(Kristine) Ilsabe Margrethe HORSTMEIER
b: 06 Feb 1771 Hille, Prussia
m: 25 Apr 1798 Hille, Prussia

Johann Carl Heinreich WEHMER
b: 25 Apr 1811 Hille, Prussia
d: 29 Jul 1866 Hille, Prussia

Caroline Marie Louise NIERMEIER
b: 18 Nov 1825 Hille, Prussia
m: 16 May 1847 Hille, Prussia
d: 13 May 1858 Hille, Prussia

Heinrich August Eduard WEHMER
b: 23 Feb 1852 Hille, Prussia
d: 05 May 1900 Florissant, MO

Sophie Marie "Louise" BUHRMESTER
b: 10 Dec 1853 Hille, Prussia
m: 23 Mar 1876 Nashville, IL
d: 02 Jan 1932 Florissant, MO

Louis (Ludwig) August WEHMER
b: 24 Oct 1886 Florissant, MO
d: 18 Aug 1952 Florissant, MO

Aurelia Ethel THOMPSON
b: 30 Jul 1887 Florissant, MO
m: 20 Mar 1913 Florissant, MO
d: 04 Dec 1976 Florissant, MO

James Henry WEHMER
b: 26 Mar 1919 Florissant, MO
d: 10 Sep 1978 Florissant, MO

Buhrmester Direct Line

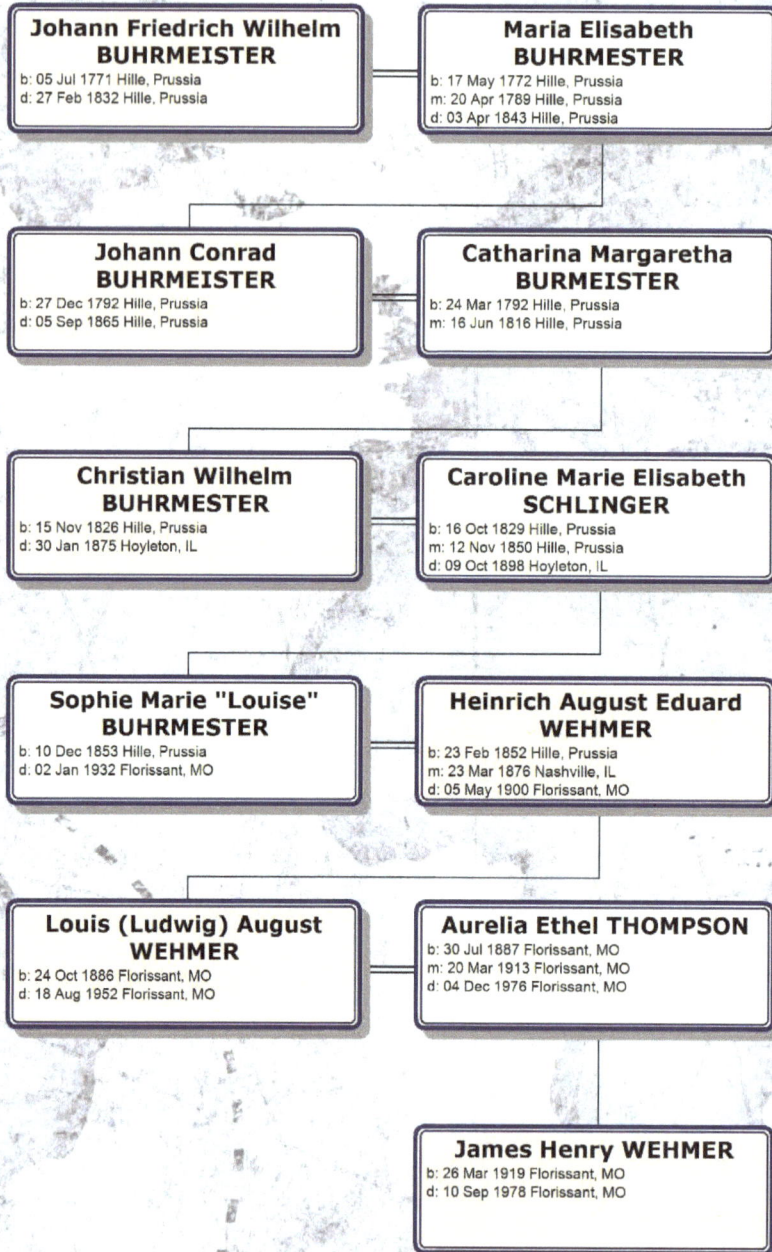

Johann Friedrich Wilhelm BUHRMEISTER
b: 05 Jul 1771 Hille, Prussia
d: 27 Feb 1832 Hille, Prussia

Maria Elisabeth BUHRMESTER
b: 17 May 1772 Hille, Prussia
m: 20 Apr 1789 Hille, Prussia
d: 03 Apr 1843 Hille, Prussia

Johann Conrad BUHRMEISTER
b: 27 Dec 1792 Hille, Prussia
d: 05 Sep 1865 Hille, Prussia

Catharina Margaretha BURMEISTER
b: 24 Mar 1792 Hille, Prussia
m: 16 Jun 1816 Hille, Prussia

Christian Wilhelm BUHRMESTER
b: 15 Nov 1826 Hille, Prussia
d: 30 Jan 1875 Hoyleton, IL

Caroline Marie Elisabeth SCHLINGER
b: 16 Oct 1829 Hille, Prussia
m: 12 Nov 1850 Hille, Prussia
d: 09 Oct 1898 Hoyleton, IL

Sophie Marie "Louise" BUHRMESTER
b: 10 Dec 1853 Hille, Prussia
d: 02 Jan 1932 Florissant, MO

Heinrich August Eduard WEHMER
b: 23 Feb 1852 Hille, Prussia
m: 23 Mar 1876 Nashville, IL
d: 05 May 1900 Florissant, MO

Louis (Ludwig) August WEHMER
b: 24 Oct 1886 Florissant, MO
d: 18 Aug 1952 Florissant, MO

Aurelia Ethel THOMPSON
b: 30 Jul 1887 Florissant, MO
m: 20 Mar 1913 Florissant, MO
d: 04 Dec 1976 Florissant, MO

James Henry WEHMER
b: 26 Mar 1919 Florissant, MO
d: 10 Sep 1978 Florissant, MO

End Notes

1 Correspondence with Lou Wehmer, son of Robert Block Wehmer, grandson of Louis Wehmer, great grandson of Heinrich Wehmer, liaison with Wehmers still in Hille, Germany.

2 Thomas Masselink "Dutch and German Words," *Masselink Genealogy (1804-2024)* (masselinkgenealogy.weebly.com).

3 Vital records for Heinrich Wehmer, his parents and siblings, at Westfalen: Landeskirchliches Archiv der Evangelischen Kirche, *Hille,* Germany (www.archion.de).

4 William L. Thomas, *History of St. Louis County, Missouri,* "Henry Wehmer profile" (St. Louis: S. J. Clarke Publishing Co., 1911), 86.

5 *History of Prussia* (Columbia, SC: Captivating History, 2021), 45-46.

6 Yasemin Nuhoglu Soysal and David Strang, "Construction of the First Mass Education Systems in Nineteenth-Century Europe," *Sociology of Education,* 62:4 (October 1989), 277-288 (jstor.org).

7 Thomas, *History of St. Louis County, Missouri,* 86.

8 Gordon Craig, *The Politics of the Prussian Army: 1640-1945* (London: Oxford University Press.1964), *7.*

9 H. W. Koch, *A History of Prussia* (New York: Barnes & Noble Books, 1978), 100.

10 Cody Franchetti, "Frederick's 'Greatness,'" *International Review of Social Sciences and Humanities,* 5:2 (2013), 160 (philarchive.org).

11 Jesse Beckett, "The Potsdam Giants: A Prussian Infantry Regiment of Nothing But Very Tall Soldiers," *War History Online,* 20 Sep 2021 (warhistoryonline.com).

12 Friedrich Müller, "Westphalian Emigrants in the 19th Century, Emigration from the Administrative District of Minden, Part II, Secret Emigration 1814 – 1900" (FamilySearch.org).

13 "Weser," *The Ship's List* (theshipslist.com).

14 Alison Clarke, "All at Sea: Childbirth on Nineteenth Century Immigrant Voyages to New Zealand," *New Zealand Journal of History,* 50:1 (2016), 18 (nzjh.auckland.ac.nz).

15 Petra DeWitt, "Early German Immigration: 1820-1860," *Show Me Missouri* (showmemo.org).

16 "Population history of St. Louis from 1830 – 1990," Boston University (physics.bu.edu).

17 "Heritage," *Anheuser-Busch* (anheuser-busch.com).

18 Helaine Silverman, Paul Kapp and Devin Hunter, "German History in Illinois," *Mythic Mississippi Project,* (mythicmississippi.illinois.edu).

19 Patrick Young, "The Germans Save St. Louis for the Union," *Long Island Wins,* 6 May 2011 (longislandwins.com).

20 "German Immigration," *A Preservation Plan for St. Louis, Part I: Historic Contexts;* 9 - Peopling St. Louis: the Immigration Experience (stlouis-mo.gov).

21 Sesquicentennial Committee of the Washington County Historical Society, *This is Washington County; its first 150 years, 1818-1968* (Nashville, IL: Washington County Historical Society, 1968), 32-33.

22 1870 U. S. Federal Census, Henry Wehmer, St. Louis, MO (Ancestry.com).

23 Buhrmester birth records, "Deutschland Geburten und Taufen, 15; 58-1898," Evangelisch, Hille, Westfalen, Prussia (Ancestry.com).

24 Tatyana Gordeeva "German Names -- Vornamen," *German Culture* (germanculture.com).

25 "Salem Lutheran, Black Jack, Baptisms," *St. Louis Genealogical Society* (stlgs.org).

26 David T. Bunch, *A History of the Salem Baptist Church,* 15 Sep 1957; Also Salem Baptist Church minutes, church history files, 3 Sep 1898.

27 Correspondence with Norman Wehmer, son of Henry Wehmer and grandson of Heinrich August Wehmer. Norman's home was near the Wehmer family Douglas Road homestead.

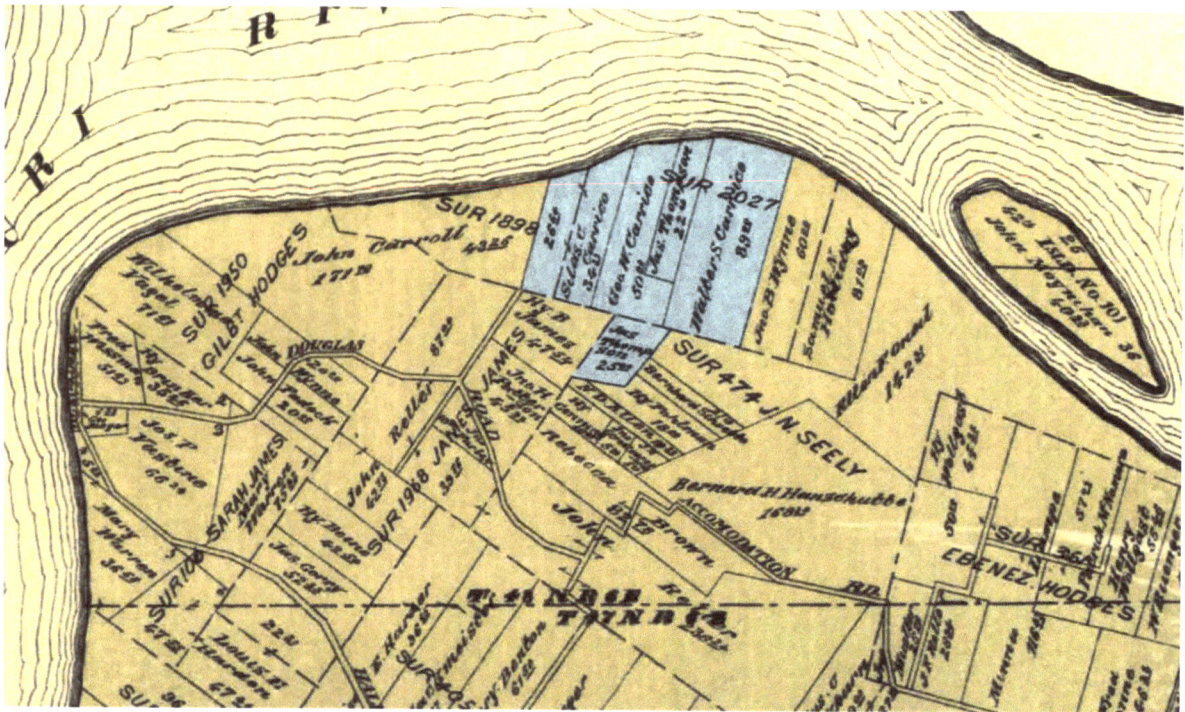

This 1893 plat map includes the Possum Hollow area bordering the Missouri River in St. Louis County. Blue shaded area represents Carrico and Thompson land.

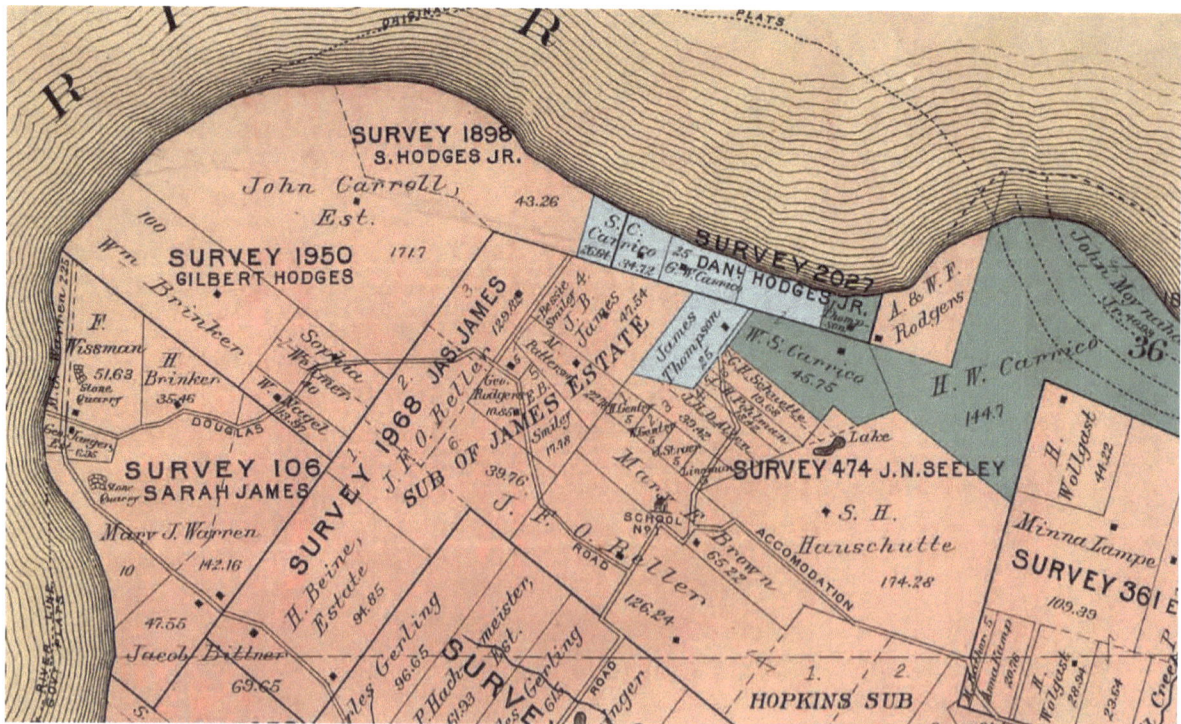

The same blue shaded area on this 1909 plat map shows what remained after the river devoured much of Carrico and Thompson lands. Green area represents acquisitions made immediately after losing much of their original land. Over the next 30 years, more than half of the land on this map belonged to Carricos, Thompsons, Wehmers and associated families.

Part Two

Samuel Riggs Snoddy and Ruth Gordon Fife, ca. 1918.

The Time-Honored Clockmaker

Samuel Riggs Snoddy
and Ruth Gordon Fife

Samuel Riggs Snoddy came from a family that believed in duty, honor and country. Sam's great great grandfather, Capt. John Snoddy, provided leadership during the Revolutionary War. His great grandfather, Joseph Walker Snoddy, served in the War of 1812. Three of Joseph Walker's sons fought for the Confederacy during America's Civil War. And Sam saw action in France during World War I, participating in the historic Meuse-Argonne campaign.

Born in 1896 to George Foster Snoddy and Nannie Riggs Snoddy of Armstrong, Missouri, Sam had one brother and four sisters. While growing up, Sam helped in his father's lumberyard when possible. He learned early to enjoy the feel of wood, and his father taught him techniques for working with it. This became a lifelong love and an avocation maintained well into retirement. When Sam reached 18 he attended school in Kirksville,

Missouri, then called First District Normal School, about 80 miles from home. Classes honed his skills in drafting, woodworking, furniture construction, machinery design and forge work.[1] After two years at Kirksville, he set out for St. Louis, where he became a salesclerk for Carleton Dry Goods Company at 12th and Washington in the city's heart. Extensive streetcar routes made it easy to commute nearly ten miles from where he lived on Page Boulevard. Just a few weeks before Sam's 21st birthday in May 1917, his draft registration card described him as medium build with gray eyes and light brown hair.[2] Four months later, World War I deferred any future plans, and he began military service at Camp Doniphan, adjacent to Ft. Sill in Oklahoma. There he trained as a field artillery mechanic assigned to the 128th Field Artillery Regiment, 60th Field Artillery Brigade, 35th Infantry Division. Men from the National Guards of Kansas and Missouri comprised this division. Draftees

Sam Snoddy taking a break in front of his tent at Camp Doniphan, Oklahoma.

added from both states brought the unit to full division strength of 27,000 men. It included two infantry brigades, a field artillery brigade and auxiliary units. The field artillery brigade included the 128th, 129th and 130th field artillery regiments.[3] One of Sam's fellow trainees, Harry S. Truman of Lamar, Missouri, served in the 129th.

Seven months at Camp Doniphan gave the men a taste of grueling conditions ahead of them on the Western Front. Fierce winds blew across the plains; dust storms temporarily blinded them as they attempted to drill, and canvas tents provided little protection against harsh winter conditions. Most days they worked from Reveille at 5:45 a.m. to Taps at 10 p.m. digging trenches, building physical endurance, setting up artillery and learning tactical use of bayonets, hand grenades and gas masks from French and British instructors.

On May 20, 1918, Sam and others in the 35th Division shipped out aboard *Saxonia*, bound for England,[4] then on to France, crossing the English Channel at night. Not long after their arrival they found themselves back in artillery school where Americans became acquainted with the mighty French gun formally known as Model 1897 75mm Cannon. A closely guarded French military secret, this gun was used throughout coming offensives. Known for its accuracy, mobility and dependability, the rapid-fire cannon advanced their earlier weapons training. Prior to the field artillery regiments' arrival in France, an elite cadre had been sent ahead to become knowledgeable about this French gun and other weaponry to instruct the full artillery brigade. Trainers included future President Truman, who had been promoted to captain and elected commanding officer of Battery D in the 129th Field Artillery regiment.[5] Corporal Sam Snoddy remembered him as a bespectacled, slightly built man who commanded the respect of those who served with him.

By mid-August the 35th Division headed east across France by train, arriving in the Vosges Mountains near Verdun. Enemy action in this area was light, but it gave them time to become accustomed to being under enemy fire and develop proficiency with weaponry. They didn't remain there for long. Orders came from Supreme Allied Command to move to the front and take part in what became known as the Meuse-Argonne Offensive. It was the largest operation of the American Expeditionary Forces (AEF) in World War I. More than a million American soldiers participated. Military historians called it the deadliest campaign in American history to that time. The fight resulted in more than 26,000 soldiers killed in action and more than 120,000 total casualties.[6] To reach its assigned sector, the 35th Division had to move from one end of the Western Front to the other in miserable weather and in what artillery historian James B. Agnew called "one of the most prodigious and exhausting road marches ever devised in modern warfare."[7] This march north took

place at night, with guns and horses hidden in timber or camouflaged during the day to avoid being spotted by German planes. Men suffered from exhaustion, and horses essential to pulling artillery caissons (two-wheeled vehicles for carrying ammunition) became worn out. Roughly 20 percent of the horses died or had to be put down during their arduous trek.[8]

Troops and surviving animals reached their position near the Argonne Forest and launched an offensive at daybreak on Sept. 26, 1918. The 35th Division had been assigned to capture Vauquois Hill, a German fortress with deep concrete dugouts and barbed wire protecting an extensive trench system.[9] French troops had been unsuccessful for four years in

The 128th Field Artillery Regiment departing Oklahoma to head overseas. Sam Snoddy is at right in the middle train window.

taking this hill. It stood along the Hindenburg Line, a German defensive position that ran north to south, along the entire Western Front.

Deafening fire from both sides filled the air and shells rained down with "whiz bangers" coming at rapid speed. One soldier supposedly asked another, "What is a whiz banger?" The reply came back, "If you hear the whiz but not the bang, you are dead. But if you hear the whiz, followed by the bang, you have lived to fight another day."[10] By 6:30 a.m, infantry of the 35th Division went over the top, and orders came for artillery to move forward.[11]

Bringing artillery along proved especially difficult because caissons had to be pulled over ground they had just shelled. Huge craters slowed their movements, including one 30 feet deep and 160 feet wide. Impassable roads made it impossible to get food and supplies through to the men, and in some cases they resorted to taking ration packs from dead soldiers.[12] In later remarks in Washington, D.C., Gen. Peter E. Traub, commander of the 35th Division in the Argonne, said:

In five days and five nights my division advanced . . . for a distance of 12 and one-half kilometers [nearly eight miles], taking positions that had baffled the French four years and which they had pronounced impregnable. They advanced in the most exposed sector of the entire battle front against artillery fire concentrated on them

Sam Snoddy and other men of the 35th Field Artillery, including a regiment led by Harry S. Truman, marched more than 100 miles over muddy back roads to play a key role in the Meuse-Argonne Offensive. Above, teams of reluctant horses and mules hauled the division's French 75 mm cannons, other artillery pieces and wagon loads of ammunition and supplies over rough and sometimes impassable terrain that required rerouting. (World War I Centennial Commission)

. . . and did it at a loss of life that under the circumstances of the battle was marvelously low. My men did what they were told to do.[13]

On Nov. 3rd, after heavy losses from a gas attack, another division relieved the 35th, though artillery units, including Sam's, stayed to provide support for replacement infantry.[14] They didn't remain in the field long, however, as fighting ceased and an Armistice was signed on Nov. 11, 1918. The Commander-in-Chief of American Expeditionary Forces, Gen. John J. Pershing, wrote in his report on the Meuse-Argonne Offensive:

> *In the chill rain of dark nights our engineers had to build new roads across spongy, shell torn areas, repair broken roads beyond No Man's Land, and build bridges. Our gunners, with no thought of sleep, put their shoulders to wheels and drag-ropes to bring their guns through the mire in support of the infantry now under the increasing fire of the enemy's artillery. Our attack had taken the enemy by surprise, but, quickly recovering himself, he began fierce counter attacks in strong force supported by heavy bombardments with large quantities of gas. Finally, I pay the supreme tribute to our officers and soldiers of the line. When I think of their heroism, their patience under hardship, their unflinching spirit of offensive action, I am filled with emotion which I am unable to express.*

Their deeds are immortal, and they have earned the eternal gratitude of our country.[15]

Corporal Sam Snoddy and other men who fought valiantly were on their way home by April 1919. They traveled from Brest, France, aboard *Vedic*, an ocean liner requisitioned as a troopship before she could begin passenger service. They arrived in Boston Harbor to great fanfare. Upon reaching St. Louis, Sam's 128th Field Artillery paraded through the city, home to most of the unit's men. In the downtown district, crowds swelled to such numbers that squad columns had to march single file in places.[16] When Harry Truman became President 25 years later, he reflected:

> *As a veteran of the First World War, I have seen death on the battlefield. When I fought in France with the 35th Division, I saw good officers and men fall and be replaced.... I know the strain, the mud, the misery [and] the utter weariness of the soldier in the field. And I know too his courage, his stamina, his faith in his comrades, his country and himself.*[17]

With war service behind him, Sam went home to Armstrong and married Ruth Gordon Fife, daughter of Leon Forest Fife and Cecile Denny Fife of Armstrong. Ruth was the third of seven children, including five girls and two boys. Her oldest sister, Anabel, died at age 14 of diphtheria, causing the Armstrong public school to close several days for fear of contagion.[18]

Ruth Gordon Fife (Snoddy)

Ruth and her siblings grew up in a large brick house known as Redstone Hall, acquired in 1871 by her grandparents, Clifton and Mary Belle Denny. Her refined environment included being sent to Hardin College and Music Conservatory, a junior college for females in Mexico, Missouri. Women there learned "graceful bearing, gentle modesty, and kind consideration which are the invariable accompaniments of good breeding," according to its 1916-1917 bulletin. It further promised that young ladies would have opportunities for "social culture and the acquirement of that grace of manner which can result only from refined and intelligent association."[19]

Apparently, Ruth learned her lessons well because those who knew her considered Ruth quite proper and stylish. Her hair turned completely white at an early age, as did her sister Cecile's, so Ruth used a blue rinse and her sister a purple rinse, putting them well ahead of their times.

The Snoddys' first child came in March 1922, and they named her Hazel Marie, after Sam's sister who died at age 18. Ten years later they had a son, Samuel Riggs Snoddy Jr. Sam Sr. and Ruth occasionally called on Hazel to let her little brother tag along when she went out with friends. For the most part, however, Hazel didn't do much around the house. Her mother had her own way of doing things and did not allow Hazel to make her own bed, wash dishes, help with household chores or cook. Even in her twenties, Hazel attempted to bake cookies for her fiancé in the Marines, but her mother shooed Hazel out of the kitchen and made them herself. Throughout Sam's and Ruth's married life he worked as a salesman for Rust Sash and Door Company and later Ash Grove Lime and Portland Cement Company.[20] Being a salesman meant they lived in a number of Missouri towns.

When Hazel married James H. Wehmer and began having children, the Snoddys did not fit a Norman Rockwell vision of grandparents. They seemed somewhat uncomfortable and reserved but had few opportunities to be around grandchildren. Their only son, Sam, had no children, and their daughter and son-in-law and their 12 children lived 250 miles away in St. Louis County, a long trip with no interstate at the time. Sometimes, however, the older children spent extended periods with the Snoddys, usually while Hazel birthed another baby.

Above, Sam and Ruth Snoddy with their children, Hazel and Sam R. Jr., 1931. Below left, Sam Snoddy with his first grandson, James Alan Wehmer, 1947; Below right, Ruth Snoddy with her first granddaughter, Ruth Anne Wehmer (the Author), 1947.

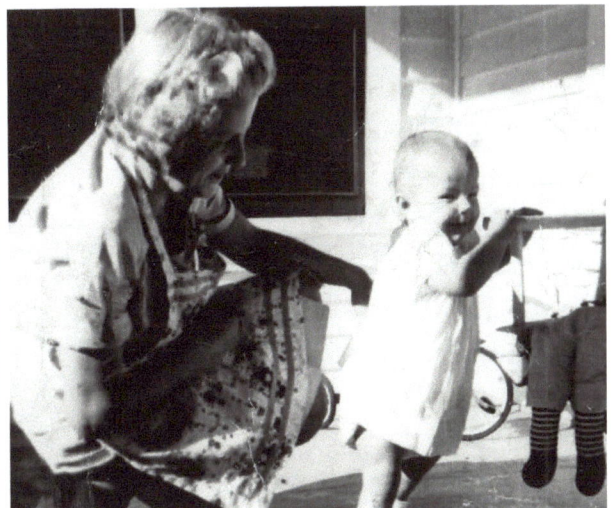

Sam Snoddy in his home workshop. This Columbia Daily Tribune *photo accompanied an article titled, "Making Clock Cases Fills Area Man's Time."* (The Columbia Daily Tribune, *photographer Len Lahman).*

At least once a year the Wehmer family drove to the Fife homeplace in Armstrong to visit Snoddy and Fife relatives. Ruth Snoddy and her three sisters returned regularly for stays with their mother, Cecile Fife, their bachelor brother who lived at home, and their youngest brother Cliff, who lived near the big house with his family. Spending a night at the Fife home made it clear why Ruth Fife Snoddy would not let her own daughter do anything around the house as she grew up. If anyone made their beds or washed the breakfast dishes, Cecile Fife, well past 90, would redo everything, warning that she wanted to do things her way.

Though unable to spend much time with their grandchildren, the Snoddys had a dog named Dede to spoil. Every evening they walked her to the Dairy Queen a block or so away from their home in Carthage and got her an ice cream cone. Eventually, its owner suggested that since Dede knew the way there, he could issue her a credit card to wear on her collar so she could come on her own. The owner looked for Dede each evening, fed her the cone and charged her account.

Upon his retirement Sam and Ruth moved to Fayette, just a short distance from where both grew up in Armstrong. Sam spent his remaining life pursuing his woodworking hobby. He began making grandfather clocks after Ruth suggested they would make unusual Christmas gifts for their son and daughter. His passion became more than a hobby. Instead of two clocks for his children, he made more than 50 clocks that went to homes in Missouri, Arkansas, Oklahoma, Kansas, Iowa and Illinois. Each required about 150 hours of work.[21]

Ruth Snoddy died of cancer in 1980 after they had been married 60 years. Not used to being alone, Sam began going to a senior center, where he met Essie Amick, who had outlived two husbands. They married at the ripe ages of 86 and 84 to keep each other company. Sam died not long thereafter in 1986.

In years before Sam's and Ruth's deaths, the Wehmers visited them in Fayette much more often. One thing remained the same whenever visits took place. Sam, the man who endured great hardships and loss while serving at the front in World War I, always stood at his door and cried when Hazel left with her family to go back to St. Louis. Hazel remained forever a daddy's girl.

Ruth and Sam Snoddy stroll along a downtown sidewalk in the early 1960s. Ruth's many pairs of pedal pushers and ankle pants were staples of her wardrobe.

Sam and Ruth Snoddy Family

Hazel Marie Snoddy

b. 25 Mar 1922, Armstrong, MO
m. James Henry Wehmer
   25 Nov 1944, Florissant, MO
d. 2 Sep 1995, Florissant, MO

Samuel Riggs Snoddy Jr.

b. 11 Jul 1931, Armstrong, MO
m. Rose Ann Carol Nevers
   1 Jul 1956, Carthage, MO
d. 29 Aug 2017, Overland Park, KS

Married 14 Apr 1920
Glasgow, MO

Ruth Gordon Fife

b. 16 Jun 1898, Armstrong, MO
d. 24 Oct 1980, Fayette, MO

Samuel Riggs Snoddy

b. 2 May 1896, Armstrong, MO
d. 7 Jun 1986, Fayette, MO

End Notes

1 Bulletin of the First District Normal School, Kirksville, Mo, June 1917, June 1916, June 1915 (mobius-vital.iii.com).

2 Samuel R. Snoddy WWI draft registration, Prairie Township, Howard County, MO (Fold3.com).

3 Connelley, William E., *History of Kansas: State and People, Volume II* (Chicago: The American Historical Society: 1928), 889-89; "World War I: the 35th Infantry Division," *Museum of the Kansas National Guard* (kansasguardmuseum.com).

4 U.S. Army WWI Transport Service, Passenger List, Samuel R. Snoddy (Fold3.com).

5 David McCullough, *Truman* (New York: Simon & Schuster, 1992), 113-119.

6 "The Meuse-Argonne Offensive," National Archives, Washington, DC (Archives.gov).

7 Robert F. Dorr, "Harry S. Truman's Battery D, 129th Field Artillery, 35th Division," *Warfare History Network*, November 2013 (warfarehistorynetwork.com).

8 Ibid.

9 Leslie L. Bucklew, compiler, *The "Orphan Battery" and Operations, 128th U.S. Field Artillery* (Cleveland, Ohio: Howard M. White, Publisher, 1921), 75.

10 Ibid., 83.

11 Ibid., 77.

12 Ibid., 77-79.

13 Ibid., 85-86.

14 Ibid., 94.

15 Ibid., 86-92.

16 Ibid., 111-112.

17 Dorr, "Harry S. Truman's Battery D."

18 Anabel Fife death, *Moberly Monitor-Index*, Moberly, MO, 16 Nov 1905 (Newspapers.com).

19 Hardin Jr. College, *Hardin College and Conservatory of Music [Catalog]*: 1911/12-1916/17, Mexico, MO (archive.org).

22 Personal information on the Snoddys is from family interviews, recollections and observances.

23 Martha Eikermann, "The time-honored clockmaker: Sam Snoddy," *Booneville Daily News,* July 21, 1980, 6D-7D.

Aurelia Thompson and Louis Wehmer on their wedding day, March 23, 1913.

To Make You Ask Questions

Louis August Wehmer
and Aurelia Ethel Thompson

When Louis A. Wehmer and Aurelia "Rill" Thompson, both of Florissant, Missouri, announced they planned to marry, her father didn't like the idea. Mr. Thompson supposedly groused that his future son-in-law was going to carry her off to a log cabin and starve her to death. Never mind that Rill's father, a Scottish immigrant, and Louis's father, a German immigrant, also started out with nothing. But a crude log cabin was no exaggeration since Louis was a young man of limited means. However, he didn't intend to stay that way. Louis learned hard work and sacrifices from an early age. These qualities would keep Rill from starving and eventually turn them into a prosperous couple. At age 13, Louis began helping his mother and brothers run their family farm in Florissant after his father died in 1900. With eight children in their family, including a baby less than one year old, their widowed mother had little time for field work. Farm chores became a priority for older children, with school attendance allowed only after planting and harvesting seasons. Nevertheless, Louis managed to complete eight years of school. To further supplement family income, he bought an Avery Steam Threshing Machine at the 1904 St. Louis World's Fair and began helping neighbors during wheat harvests.* Most likely Louis learned this skill from James Thompson, a respected wheat thresher who, unbeknownst at the time, would become his father-in-law.

---

* Wheat harvesting includes cutting (or reaping) wheat, then threshing to separate edible grain from straw. Later farm equipment included both functions on one machine, thus called a "combine."

Preparing for wheat harvest with the threshing machine Louis bought at the 1904 World's Fair.

Like Louis, Rill grew up in a large family, eighth of nine living children. She experienced a different childhood, however, being spoiled by her parents and older siblings. At age six Rill started at the one-room Brown School (then called James School) where she completed seven years. In her eighties, Rill recalled it vividly:

> *We had a well in front with two wooden buckets on a chain. My, how those boys would delight in dousing me with water when I walked by. There was a chimney at each end [of the school] and a pot belly stove on one end only. I'd burn up on one side and freeze on the other. . . There were blackboards at each end of the room and double seats - two children for each desk. We had no cloakroom – hooks on the wall did the job. The windowsills held our sack lunches.*[1]

Not wanting to take an arduous examination that came at the end of eighth grade in county schools, Rill moved in with a brother who lived in St. Louis. She completed her elementary education there, then started at Central High School, established in 1853 as the first public school west of the Mississippi River. Central remained the only secondary school in St. Louis until overcrowding forced the city to build two new schools.[2] Yeatman opened in 1904, and Rill transferred to this state-of-the-art facility in the city's North end and nearer to home. Named for a St. Louis business leader, the school included a gymnasium, 1,000-seat auditorium, restrooms on upper floor levels and shower/bath facilities.[3] It was a world apart from the school where Rill started. The one-room school still had an outhouse more than 20 years later when her sons attended.

After returning home to Florissant from downtown St. Louis, Rill became active in Salem Baptist Church, their family place of worship just across the street from Brown School. Youth activities became much more interesting after Louis, a year older, started flirting with her. They married on Easter morning, 1913. Church records indicate that she looked lovely in a pale blue chiffon dress over pale blue silk and carried a bouquet of roses. A supportive congregation wished them happiness and prosperity, and they became one of the church's most outstanding young couples.[4] After an "elegant" dinner at the bride's home less than a mile from church, Louis donned his sporty straw boater, hitched his mules to a wagon, and drove his bride to their log cabin. Others noted their marriage as well. Though Louis was born in this country, his parents maintained ties with their native Prussia. Louise Wehmer made sure her son and his bride-to-be appeared under a marriage registration column headed "Heirathsicheine" in *Westliche Post*, St. Louis's primary German newspaper.[5]

Louis and Rill led a simple life and, despite her father's concerns, the farm kept them supplied with plenty of food for their growing family of four boys. Their sons helped with farmwork, but sometimes forgot that agricultural equipment could be dangerous. On one occasion, while playing around a corn grinder, which operated somewhat like a merry-go-round, five-year-old Ralph put his hand into the grinder and lost part of a finger. Many years later he recalled his trip in the family's Model-T to reach the nearest doctor. "Because the

Four generations of Wehmer baptisms, marriages and funerals took place in Salem Baptist Church, shown here in 1910.

road was dirt and full of ruts, we hitched it to a team of mules, and we headed to Salem Baptist Church with the reins through the windshield opening. We left the mules at the church where the road began and drove on into Florissant to the doctor's office."[6]

Wehmer boys also had some memorable moments at Brown School. Ralph described a particularly strange day:

> One foggy morning about 8:30 a. m., while outside at school, we heard a noise that caught our attention. . . We saw a bi-plane flying low about 50 feet above our heads. The pilot circled, cut the engine, and hollered, "Where's the nearest airport?" We kids made a "human arrow" pointed to the airport in Anglum, now Lambert International Airport. The pilot circled around and yelled down, "Thank you!" The person in the plane happened to be Charles Lindbergh! We could even see his flight jacket.[7]

The log cabin in Possum Hollow where Louis and Rill lived after their marriage and raised their sons.

At that time fog lights placed every ten miles led pilots to the airport, but it was so foggy that morning he couldn't see to fly the last leg of his air mail route. Lindbergh had been hired by a St. Louis corporation in October 1925 to map out and serve as chief pilot for a newly designated 278-mile mail route. He and three other pilots flew mail between St. Louis and Chicago with stops in Springfield and Peoria, Illinois, in a fleet of modified war-surplus bi-planes.[8] Lindbergh flew the route until 1931, taking time out for his famous Paris flight in 1927. That same year, he dipped his wings over Brown School.

During their marriage's early years, Louis proved his worth as a farmer through sound agricultural practices and a keen business sense. With America's entry into World War in 1917, demand for farm products increased significantly, and he began to establish a family reserve fund to eventually build a new house and expand their farm. Though Louis registered for selective service, the country needed him to perform his patriotic duty in fields closer to home. With Europe at war, producing large harvests became vital for sustaining the more than 4.7 million American military personnel, along with overseas allies. Just days after Woodrow Wilson declared war in early April 1917, the President asked American farmers to produce more foodstuffs, calling it as important as military service. Wilson's message said in part:

> *The supreme need of our own nation and of the nations with which we are co-operating is an abundance of supplies, and*

especially of food-stuffs. . . . Without abundant food, alike for the armies and the peoples now at war, the whole great enterprise upon which we have embarked will break down and fail. The world's food reserves are low. Not only during the present emergency but for some time after peace shall have come both our own people and a large proportion of the people of Europe must rely upon the harvests in America. Upon the farmers of this country, therefore, in large measure, rests the fate of the war and the fate of the nations.[9]

Wilson called upon housewives as well to grow large gardens and avoid wastefulness in their households. "Every housewife who practices strict economy puts herself in the ranks of those who serve the nation," he said. The Wehmer family served their country's war effort, raising wheat, corn and alfalfa, along with beef and dairy cattle, hogs, sheep and chickens. With demand soaring, crop prices skyrocketed, and average value of a Missouri farm rose from $49.61 per acre in 1910 to $88.08 per acre by war's end.[10]

But things did not remain favorable for American farmers. As prices of their products soared during the war, some farmers borrowed money to buy more acres and new equipment they couldn't afford. National farm mortgages doubled between 1910 and 1920, from $3.3 billion to $6.7 billion.[11] By the early 1920s, European countries previously at war resumed farm production, flooding world markets. Oversupply caused prices to plunge, leading to inability of some to pay off mortgages or finance crop loans. Fortunately, Louis had not mortgaged any land and had built up his savings significantly during boom years. After the 1929 Stock Market Crash, however, his asset values dwindled to almost nothing, and he had to redouble his efforts to provide for his family. This "Black Tuesday"* crash reverberated throughout the entire economy, and by the early 1930s many farmers received less for their crops than it cost to produce them. Corn prices dropped from a high of $1.45 per bushel during the war to a low of 29 cents per bushel by 1932. Wheat went from $2.45 per bushel in 1920 down to 49 cents in 1932. And the value of Missouri farmland dropped from its wartime high average of $88.08 to $31.36 per acre in 1935.[12]

To add to this misery, a drought in 1930 burned up crops in fields or made it impossible to plant a crop. Rainfall that year in Missouri reached only 78 percent of the average mean, with 85 percent being considered drought conditions. The St. Louis area also had experienced a severe drought in 1901, the year after Louis's father died. The 15-year-old Louis, along with his brothers, worked hard to keep their family farm operational when rainfall in Missouri registered 63 percent of the average mean.[13] So he knew from experience that they had to tighten belts and intensify efforts to make it through crippling dry spells. While not as hard

---

* *Black Tuesday refers to Tuesday, Oct. 29, 1929, the day stock market prices fell sharply, signaling start of the Great Depression.*

hit as Missouri's western sections, the 1930s drought and dust kept Louis and his family out of fields for long periods. But there was little they could do, other than wait it out. The son of one Missouri farmer who weathered such a drought recalled, "I would go to the fields with my father each day and see the look of desperation on his face. It's gut-wrenching to watch your crops wither and know that you're helpless to do anything about it."[14]

Some farmers did not survive this crisis and lost their income and farms. Children's book author Karen Hesse, writing about the Dust Bowl, noted, "Hard times aren't only about money, or drought, or dust. Hard times are about losing spirit, and hope, and what happens when dreams dry up." Louis Wehmer never lost sight of his dreams and continued to maintain a normal life for his family. While waiting to get back in their fields, they took an opportunity to visit Rill's sister and her husband, Sarah and Horace Wagner. The Wagners had gone west after their marriage in 1909 and established a ranch in Reliance, South Dakota.

Unfortunately, a catastrophic insect invasion followed the Wehmers on their trip westward. At the end of July 1931, Missouri's *Springfield Press* reported, "Ravenous grasshoppers of a nonmigratory but exceptionally greedy variety swarmed in wriggling hordes Wednesday over more than 46,875 square miles of farm lands in five middle western states and caused damage of which crop experts could say only that 'it will run into the millions.'"[15] By the time Louis, Rill and the boys reached South Dakota, its governor had declared an emergency, announcing that "grasshoppers have utterly destroyed all crops in 11,000 square miles of South Dakota."[16] The Wehmers' youngest son, Bob, recalled that when they arrived at the Wagners' ranch, grasshoppers were even devouring fenceposts.

Salvaging their trip, the Wehmers went on to the Black Hills and Mount Rushmore, where they witnessed sculptor Gutzon Borglum, son of Danish immigrants, carving out presidential faces on the side of this mountain.[17] Dedication of the George Washington figure had taken place the previous July, and Borglum was working on a Thomas Jefferson bust in 1931. While Wehmers saw Jefferson's face taking shape on Washington's right, Borglum eventually dynamited his false start and moved Jefferson to Washington's left.[18]

This trip to South Dakota may have spurred the Wehmers' later decision to bring Horace and Sarah Wagners' youngest daughter, Hazel, to live with them in St. Louis County. At that time the nearest high school in South Dakota was a great distance from the Wagners' farm, which required boarding. They already were sending one daughter and could not afford to send another. Louis Wehmer couldn't let that happen and said, "You're going to come and live with us and go to school." Hazel pitched in with household and farm chores to help with room and board.[19]

Despite adverse financial and environmental conditions, the Wehmers never suffered like many. With plenty of food on the farm, no one went hungry, and they often shared with those unable to produce crops. By the mid-1930s,

The Wehmer brothers, above from left, Jim, Bob, Ralph and Louis, spoof their pledge not to smoke or drink before age 21. All received a gold watch, such as Jim's pictured below, for honoring their commitment.

the farm economy began to turn around, thanks to President Franklin D. Roosevelt's New Deal policies to get people back on their feet. Louis moved his family out of their log cabin in 1935 and into a bungalow-style house at the end of Curlee Lane, where they lived the remainder of their lives. Louis and Rill enforced strict discipline in their family and stressed that their boys be guided by moral principles. When they became teenagers, their father promised them $100 each and a gold watch if they did not smoke or drink before age 21. All four boys made it (supposedly), and Louis kept his pledge. The boys spent the $100 and retained these watches throughout their lives.[20]

Wheat harvest time on the Wehmer farm required manual labor from their extended family in the late 1930s and early 1940s. Louis's sons often had the task of perching on top of the wagon to guide a team of draft horses. Though the above image is from an Iowa farm, this was a typical sight around St. Louis County, Missouri.

For both Louis and Rill, family meant everything, and they experienced great pride when all their children graduated from high school. After high school the Wehmers' two oldest sons, Louis and Ralph, became respected community and church leaders. Jim and Bob attended the University of Missouri, each graduating with degrees in agriculture. With World War II looming, both entered the military as commissioned officers after graduating. Jim served in the Marine Corps and Bob in the Navy. Their South Dakota niece, Hazel, married a Florissant boy and remained near Louis and Rill. When Wehmer

boys married and had children, relatives gathered for lunch every Sunday after church. Rill prepared an entrée, and each family brought a dish. Children played hide-and-seek and tag on the lawn. Adults engaged in croquet or horseshoes, visited or napped until time for evening church services. This tradition continued on Sundays and holidays until their 21 grandchildren and their niece's four children were grown.

Louis Wehmer was a kind grandfather and adored by his grandchildren. This author's recollections, like memories of other

Above left, Rill Wehmer with her sons and bonus daughter, Hazel Maxwell, ca. 1940: From left, Ralph, Hazel, Jim, Rill, Bob and Louis. Above right, Louis August Wehmer.

grandchildren old enough to remember him, include his helping them shinny up a metal basement pole, standing them on a table to keep their yo-yos from hitting the floor and allowing them to help with farm chores. When incessantly asked by his grandchildren, "Why are you doing that, Grandpa?" his standard answer became "To make little girls (or boys) ask questions." That always ended the subject.

Sometimes helping with chores didn't last long. Once his oldest granddaughter, Susan, about 5, tried helping with milking Bessie the cow. Louis showed her how to do it by squirting milk into a cat's mouth. When Susan took over, she apparently lacked the right touch, and an annoyed Bessie swished her tail in her face. Susan never helped with milking again.[20]

In his later years Louis received burns over his entire body when a tractor overturned on him. It required extensive hospitalization followed by long bedrest at home, causing great consternation among his grandchildren. They became especially concerned after hearing that the hospital packed him in a tub of ice to aid his recovery, a treatment they considered barbaric. Children were not allowed in his hospital room, so one Sunday after church all his grandchildren stood on the lawn three stories below his room. Rill wheeled him to a large window at the end of a hall so he could see his grandchildren waving at him. Louis waving back remains a vivid memory. Death of their oldest son Louis in a car accident at age 35 devastated Louis and Rill. Working as a traveling salesman in 1950, his car skidded off the road and hit a tree while he was returning to St. Louis. Some say Louis never got over his son's death. When he died just two years later the death certificate said he had a heart attack; family members believed he died of a broken heart.

Rill lived alone for more than 25 years after her husband's death, but she was more than capable of taking care of herself. Always feisty and independent, she had at least one close call. During her later years Rill walked over a cistern outside her back door, and the wooden cover gave way, dropping her into a water-filled cavern. She managed to brace herself with her feet on one wall and her elbows on the opposite wall and inched her way out. Other than bruises and cuts, she climbed out relatively unscathed. Rill recalled praying that the Lord would save her because she didn't want people to think she was despondent and committed suicide.[21]

For many years Louis and Rill had participated in a Farmers' Market on Saturdays in downtown St. Louis. Rill continued making these trips after his death and took her grandchildren, usually two at a time, to help. Other St. Louis County relatives and friends had booths, and hers occupied a prime spot in front of Perlmutter's Department Store on Grand Avenue. She had her own ways of making sure her grandkids helped rather than hindered. After they assisted in setting up her booth, she put them to work shucking corn for display and picking off any silkworms. It had to be done quickly because a man always showed up around 8 a.m. and paid a nickel for each worm, saying he wanted to fry them for breakfast. Years later her grandchildren realized that Rill was paying him to come by early and pretend he needed worms for

Rill Wehmer, on her front porch with grandson Greg (youngest son of Jim and Hazel), ca. 1969. She took care of him while Hazel worked, and the toddler accompanied his grandmother to extension club gatherings and other outings. As a result, Greg's speech patterns sounded like the elderly women he spent his days with. For example, if asked if he wanted something to eat, Greg's response typically was, "Why, yes, I think I'll have a little bite of something!!"

Grandchildren of Louis and Rill Wehmer in 2001. Wehmer grandsons from back row left: Ralph, Dave, Greg, Lyle, Louie, Jeff, Bob, Jack, Dan, Jim and Lou. Wehmer granddaughters from front row left: Ginny Borcherding, Susan Kagy, Linda Wolfe, Jean Bozoian, Ruth Hawkins, Barbara Skaggs, Lisa, Jill, Gay Cusumano. (Another grandchild, Becky Woodring, died in 1977.)

breakfast to make sure corn was free of worms and ready for sale.

Rill lived a long life and remained active almost until her death at age 89. She taught Sunday School and Vacation Bible School at Salem Baptist Church for 75 years and assisted with the church's Meals on Wheels program for shut-ins until hospitalized a month before her death. Rill was a 4-H leader, an avid member of the County Extension Homemakers Club, and served as a Democratic election commissioner for 30 years. Her obituary noted that "Mrs. Wehmer's great-great grandfather fought in the American Revolutionary War and later settled in the Florissant area. Carrico Road is named for her grandfather, Walter Carrico, who was a farmer."[23]

Louis actively participated in agricultural organizations, held church leadership positions and spent his last 12 years as secretary of the Florissant Valley Cooperative Elevator Association. Chances are, if you asked him why he chose a life of farming and living off the land, his response would be "To make you ask questions."

Louis and Aurelia Wehmer Family

Ralph Edward Wehmer

b. 26 Jan 1916, Florissant, MO
m. Rosemary Virginia Fuqua
  4 Sep 1943, Florissant, MO
d. 15 Jul 2007, Florissant, MO

James Henry Wehmer .

b. 26 Mar 1919, Florissant, MO
m. Hazel Marie Snoddy
  25 Nov 1944, Florissant, MO
d. 10 Sep 1978, Florissant, MO

Louis Silas Wehmer

b. 14 Jan 1915, Florissant, MO
d. 15 May 1950, Florissant, MO

Robert Block Wehmer

b. 22 Aug 1920, Florissant, MO
m. Marguerite P. Gauldin
  12 Oct 1951, Mountain View, MO
d. 4 April 2001, Willow Springs, MO

Louis August Wehmer

b. 24 Oct 1886, Florissant, MO
d. 18 Aug 1952, Florissant, MO

Married 23 Mar 1913
Florissant, MO

Aurelia Ethel Thompson

b. 30 Jul 1887, Florissant, MO
d. 4 Dec 1976, Florissant, MO

End Notes

[1] Gregory M. Franzwa, *History of the Hazelwood School District* (Florissant, MO: Hazelwood School District, 1977), 11.

[2] "Central High School, St. Louis, Missouri," *Historic Structures*, 9 Sep 2023 (historic-structures.com).

[3] Ibid.

[4] "A Church Wedding," *The Salem Baptist Church* news article, Florissant, MO, 23 May 1913.

[5] "Heirathsicheine," *Westliche Post*, 21 Mar 1913 (Newspapers.com).

[6] "Ralph Wehmer's Stories," recorded by daughters Susan Wehmer Kagy and Virginia Wehmer Borcherding, along with Olga S. Smith, June-July 2007.

[7] Ibid.

[8] "Lindbergh History April 1926- November 1926," *Charles Lindbergh: An American Aviator* (charleslindbergh.com).

[9] Woodrow Wilson, "Address to the Nation," *The American Presidency Project*, 16 Apr 1917 (presidency.ucsb.edu).

[10] "Agriculture: Missouri," *Bulletin, Fourteenth Census of the United States: 1920*, Bureau of the Census, Department of Commerce (census.gov).

[11] Sam Moore, "U.S. Farmers During the Great Depression," *Farm Collector*, 19 Sep 2011 (farmcollector.com).

[12] U.S. Bureau of the Census, *Historical Statistics of the United States, Colonial Times to 1957* (Washington, DC, 1960), 122-123 (u-s-history.com); and Harwood D. Schaffer and Daryll E. Ray, "Multi-year stretches of corn prices have been shaped by federal policy and world wars," *Agricultural Policy Analysis Center*, Knoxville, TN, 2019 (agpolicy.org).

[13] "Climate at a Glance County Mapping," National Centers for Environmental Information (ncei.noaa.gov).

[14] Family interviews.

[15] "Grasshoppers Devastate 47,000 Square Miles of Farm Land," *The Springfield Press*, Springfield, MO, 29 Jul 1931, 9 (newspapers.com).

[16] "South Dakota governor begs for federal assistance over grasshopper plague," *This Day in History*, 14 Jul 1931 (history.com).

[17] Robert B. Wehmer recollections, related by Barbara Wehmer Skaggs.

[18] Martin Kelly, "Interesting Mount Rushmore Facts," *ThoughtCo*, 9 Aug 2024 (thoughtco.com).

[19] Hazel Wagner Maxwell Davis memories, recalled by Ross Maxwell and Virginia Wehmer Borcherding.

[20] Susan Wehmer Kagy memories.

[21] "Ralph Wehmer's Stories."

[22] "Aurelia Wehmer Rites Today," Florissant, MO, 7 Dec 1976, unknown newspaper. Family collection.

WWII Marine fighter pilot Jim Wehmer and his wife Hazel, former TWA statistician, take to country life, including this break from cleaning out their barn.

The Sky's the Limit

James Henry Wehmer
and Hazel Marie Snoddy

Like their ancestors, James H. (Jim) Wehmer and Hazel Marie Snoddy made a long journey before settling down with each other. Jim started as a naïve country boy who became a distinguished and decorated Marine fighter pilot during World War II. Hazel began as a privileged town girl before moving to Washington D. C. as a statistician for what became Trans World Airlines. One also might say they were further proof of earlier generations' experiences that opposites attract.

Born March 26, 1919, to Louis and Rill Wehmer, Jim lived his early childhood in a log cabin at Possum Hollow, a rural area of Florissant, Missouri. Their farm included fertile land in St. Louis County. Jim and his father and brothers worked the fields, especially during planting and harvesting seasons. He went to church on Wednesday nights and twice on Sundays. He and brothers Louis, Ralph and Bob went to the same one-room Brown School that their mother had

attended. Jim's seventh grade report card displayed A's and B's, though he occasionally had trouble with deportment. School entertainments typically included both students and community residents, and Wehmer boys played their part. Brown School presented a double feature in 1935, with alums Louis, Ralph and Jim handling key roles in a three-act comedy-drama, *The Glow Lights of San Rey.* Bob entertained on harmonica between acts.

Hazel descended from several genteel old families in Kentucky who pioneered Howard County, Missouri, not long after the War of 1812. Born in Armstrong, Missouri, to Sam and Ruth Snoddy on March 25, 1922, Hazel rarely lifted a finger around the house. Her mother had a preferred way of doing things and did not want Hazel making her own bed, cleaning her room, or attempting to cook. Hazel's father took her shopping for most

Aurelia Wehmer with her son Jim in 1919.

anything she wanted, picked out all her clothes and took her to appointments and events. Hazel moved at least five times while growing up, thanks to her father's sales jobs. Wherever she lived, Hazel ran with town kids, all somewhat "wild" in that they smoked and drank. Friends called her "Red" because of her bright auburn hair, and she became part of a group of girls who called themselves "The Posse."

In fall 1933 Jim began attending John M. Vogt High School in Ferguson, Missouri, where he played on the baseball and basketball teams. Several years later Sam Snoddy and his family

relocated to Ferguson, and Hazel enrolled at Vogt High School as well. Sam loved basketball and attended nearly all the high school games in Ferguson. His daughter took note of Jim, a star basketball player, though he supposedly didn't give a second glance to this three-years-younger redheaded sophomore. His indifference eventually disappeared, however, after Jim graduated high school. He enrolled in the University of Missouri at Columbia in 1937 and found that the Snoddys had moved to Columbia. Having never been away from home before, Jim visited them often to feel less homesick and talk basketball with Sam. At that time Hazel lived at home and attended Hickman High School. Always an excellent student, she graduated as salutatorian from Hickman in 1939. That fall Hazel enrolled in Christian College (now Columbia College), then an all-girls two-year school. Her parents considered it a "finishing school," even though Hazel wasn't finished with her education.

Jim graduated with a B.S. degree in agriculture in 1941 and returned home to Florissant before entering the U.S. Marine Corps. That same year Hazel received her two-year associate of liberal arts degree from Christian and enrolled at the University of Missouri. During Jim's last two years of college he dated one of Hazel's classmates at Christian. But with everyone graduating and Jim leaving for flight training, his girlfriend stopped writing him. Jim knew Hazel well enough to ask her to intercede. Concerned that there must be someone else, he wanted Hazel to find out where he stood or if he didn't stand a chance. Hazel served as go-between for a time, but

Ferguson High School baseball team, 1935. Jim Wehmer is third from left in back row.

when Jim came home on leave, looking dapper in his dress uniform, everything changed. Hazel recalled that she had never seen anyone quite so handsome and decided to forget friendship and make her own play for him. As letters grew more frequent between Jim and Hazel, he fell in love with the redhead.

Prior to Jim's deployment overseas, Hazel graduated with a bachelor's degree in business administration in 1943 from the University of Missouri. A top student in her classes, she taught statistics during her senior year since many male faculty members had been called into wartime service. After graduation she put her skill with numbers to work by becoming a statistician for Transcontinental & Western Air, Inc., renamed Trans World Airlines in 1950. Based in its Washington, D.C. office, Hazel assisted in plotting new routes for this expanding company, then considered a major

Jim Wehmer, ca. 1935, posing in his youth equestrian program uniform.

Hazel Snoddy with her "Posse." From left, Sarah (Popeye), Hazel (Red), Anna (Sis) and Joyce (Hot Shot), ca. 1928.

airline in the United States. During her time there the airline increased its domestic routes, along with establishing its first commercial international routes.[1]

Jim completed flight training at Pensacola, Florida, then received orders in January 1943 for Cherry Point, North Carolina, to join a night fighter squadron in its development stages. Marine Corps Night Fighter Squadron 531 became the first of its kind. Though approved at the highest Marine Corps echelons, not all agreed on such use of limited resources. In fact, the authorizing directive emphasized that no materials, equipment or planes could be diverted from other units. The squadron had to equip out-of-date planes with radar and armament, learn to fly multi-engine aircraft at night, develop expertise in aircraft interception radar (AI) and set up a ground-controlled interception system (GCI) to guide planes into position for engaging targets. Training controllers to operate this system was crucial to their operations. By fall 1943 the squadron, which became known as Grey Ghosts, headed to the South Pacific. Major Frank H. Schwable, their commanding officer, cited concerns that they were sending the squadron into combat "in an airplane that is admittedly makeshift for the job, with guns that may or may not all fire, and with instruments that are difficult to read, and with radar that so far has an average of one out of three working."[2]

Problems continued after they reached the Solomon Islands, but Grey Ghosts succeeded despite them. Their night patrols resulted in dramatic decreases in threats from hostile aircraft. During its tour of duty in the Solomons, the squadron operated from bases on Russell Islands, Bougainville, and Vella Lavella, primarily covering task forces operating in the area and protecting them from observation and attack by Japanese aircraft. In addition the unit covered beach landings and protected troops from bombing and harassment after they went ashore.

Hazel Snoddy at Christian College

The squadron's deadliest day came March 21, 1944, as three pilots and their crews headed back to base after a mission. Flying in formation, one pilot clipped a second pilot's wings. The first plane exploded, and the second plane went into a tailspin and plunged into the sea. A third pilot flew low to search for signs of life but found only bits of debris. During the next 24 hours, Jim and then-commanding officer John Harshberger each piloted a search plane but failed to find the nine men who lost their lives.[3]

In May 1944, Jim was promoted to captain and became the third commanding officer of this squadron. His daily War Diary expressed continuing concern related to the GCI station. Though the squadron had its own controller, sometimes they had to use controllers on land bases or vessels being protected. Other times they placed their controller on one of the

Hazel Snoddy, right, posing with her cousin Cecile Markland, ca. 1937

vessels. This occasionally led to lack of communication, jealousy, competition and turf disputes. During one mission, for example, Jim protected a group of P.T. boats, with Grey Ghosts' squadron controller placed on one of the vessels. When communication equipment on this control boat broke down, Jim asked other boats to relay messages to his controller. They refused, complying only after Jim threatened to abandon the mission and leave them unprotected.[4] By June cooperation had improved, and Jim wrote that at no time were P.T. boats bombed by enemy planes while being covered by his night fighters.[5]

Flying night patrols could be harrowing, but sometimes quite peaceful. Enroute to one mission Jim turned controls over to the radar officer and wrote a letter to his cousin Hazel Wagner:

> We are now cruising along at 1800 feet just under a cumulus cloud cover. . . If my writing is unusually poor I'll blame it on the rough air and occasional rain showers we are going through. Off on my left we are passing a small island. Otherwise, we are pretty well surrounded by endless miles of dark blue water.[6]

Sometimes it did not go smoothly. In another letter Jim wrote that all his radios failed and he got lost. "There is a lot of water out there and the night was plenty dark. After wandering around for about an hour I finally saw some lights and flew to them and soon found out where I was."[7]

In August 1944 the squadron was recalled to Cherry Point. During their deployment in the Solomon Islands, Grey Ghosts had shot down

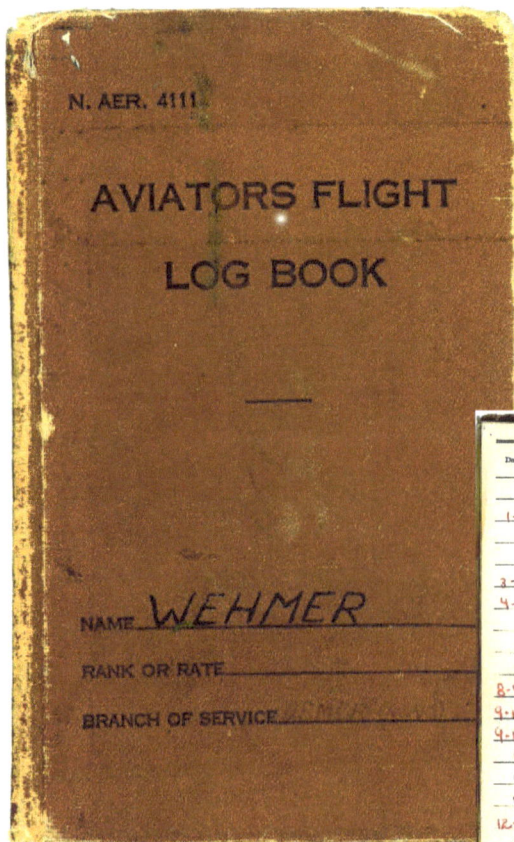

An excerpt from Jim Wehmer's flight log book.

Jim Wehmer climbs into his Corsair fighter to lead his Reserve Squadron in aerial maneuvers.

12 enemy planes, along with bombing enemy ground positions and barges used by Japanese to bring in supplies. They lost 20 men and six aircraft, though none by enemy fire.[8] Army Brig. Gen. Earl W. Barnes of the joint U.S. operational command in the Solomons commended the squadron for its pioneering work in night fighting. He noted that dramatic reduction in enemy night air activity "has been largely due to the successful effort of VMF-531 . . . with antiquated equipment . . . and an abundance of personal effort and ability of all members of the organization."[8] Jim also received personal recognition for his service. During his overseas tour he flew 71 missions, earning an Air Medal awarded by the President of the United States "for his service during operations against enemy Japanese forces in the Solomon Islands and Bismarck Archipelago Areas, from 2 December 1943 to 15 June 1944."[9]

By October 1944 the squadron had reassembled at Cherry Point as a replacement training unit with Jim as adjutant. Before setting off for additional training at Vero Beach, Florida, however, he took leave to marry Hazel on Nov. 25, 1944, at Salem Baptist Church in Florissant. She left her job with the airline and accompanied him to Vero Beach where they lived on base. Hazel had never boiled water, but she took cram courses

Hazel Snoddy and Jim Wehmer on their
wedding day, Nov. 25, 1944.

in cooking and learned how to do household tasks from other officers' wives. Fortunately, Hazel learned fast since she ultimately had 12 children to feed and raise. In January 1945 the squadron relocated to the Marine Air Corps Station at Eagle Mountain Lake, Texas, as an aviation training unit. Jim commanded this group from June until October 1945, overseeing downsizing at war's end. He received his letter of separation from active duty at the end of December and returned to civilian life.[11]

The couple's oldest son, James Alan, was born in Edina, Missouri, where Jim worked as an agricultural extension agent during his first year after active service. Many offers came for him

to be a commercial pilot, but farming remained his love and generational heritage. He soon came home to assist on his dad's farm and put his agricultural degree to use by applying scientific farming methods. His projects included designing and implementing contour plowing techniques to prevent soil erosion through a system of waterways and terraces. The system became a county demonstration project.[12]

Jim and Hazel and their son lived with his parents when they first moved back to Florissant, along with a second child, Ruth Anne (the author). By 1949 he acquired his own farm, a 162-acre property adjacent to his father's land along Accommodation Road (later Old Jamestown Road) on bluffs above the Missouri River. Learning to live in a drafty, two-story house on their farm -- with limited heat, no running water and no plumbing -- proved difficult for Hazel. A wood-burning stove in the dining room, which also served as a family gathering place, provided the only heat. During winters children slept on pallets around the stove for warmth, often sharing space with runt litters of pigs or premature calves that Jim brought in to keep warm. Children slept on those same pallets during summer with a large fan blowing. Even though the family expanded to nine children while living in this house, four of the six rooms went largely unused. The living room typically remained closed off to concentrate heat in the dining room, except at Christmas when a tree was erected in that room. Two upstairs bedrooms remained too hot or too cold and rarely saw use. A third upstairs room held stored and discarded items. Along with running a huge household, Hazel loved activities such as sewing, working with crafts and planning get-togethers for former Marine friends and a St. Louis chapter of the Christian College Alumnae Association. She never tired of special projects associated with Christmas. Hazel loved baking and decorating cookies, making personalized stockings for her children, decorating holiday ornaments and buying and wrapping presents. She spent hours finding exactly the right wrap for each child's gifts. There were lots of other Christmas traditions, including not purchasing a tree until Christmas Eve and decorating it as a family. Afterward, Jim gathered everyone around and read the Christmas story from the Bible. This tradition sometimes led to innovations. For example, if trees looked totally picked over by Christmas Eve, Jim bought two trees—one tall and skinny, the other short and fat. He cut branches off the short tree and stuck them into holes that he drilled into the tall tree.

For 14 years after active service Jim remained in the reserves and commanded Marine Air Reserve Squadron 221 at Lambert Field in St. Louis. When the squadron went on maneuvers, Jim sometimes flew over the farmhouse and dipped his wings. His children would climb up to flat boards atop the fence surrounding a pig pen when they saw him approaching. They wanted to get as close as possible to wave. Sometimes it seemed like they could touch his wings if they stretched their arms skyward far enough. In a *St. Louis Post Dispatch* feature article about Jim flying while being a full-time farmer, he tried to explain his love of flight: "Maybe it'll sound corny, but when you get up there by yourself, with all the world under you, for a little while you're king of the whole business. You're free."[13]

Jim Wehmer demonstrating contour plowing on his father's farm.

Jim and Hazel Wehmer farmstead on Old Jamestown Road, Florissant, ca. 1955.

In 1959 Jim and Hazel sold their farm and built a modern, split-level home just across the road from their old farmhouse. Hazel started from scratch when they made the move and did not take a single piece of furniture from the farmhouse. She loved picking out all new furniture and adding special elements, such as a brick entrance hall, walnut paneling milled from the farm, radiant heat on the lower level and a grandfather clock and furniture for two bedrooms made by her father. Two logs from Jim's birthplace cabin were salvaged to create mantels for their living room and family room fireplaces. Along with farming, Jim worked other jobs to keep his large family fed— salesman for a livestock feed company, shoe repair shop owner, grain elevator operator, driver for cars coming off the Ford assembly line in Hazelwood, Missouri, and plant operations manager for a quarry on the Missouri River. Hazel became office manager at the same quarry where Jim worked. On one occasion Jim's boss tasked him with implementing a zoned pay plan for hauling rock that would have adversely affected black drivers. He refused to do so and quit on the spot. It was a courageous stand, but not very practical for a man with many mouths to feed.

For the first time in Jim's life, he had to fill out job applications and suffer the humiliation of jobs being given to younger men. Despite these dark days, his stance ultimately won out when he landed a similar job with a bigger salary at a nearby quarry. Hazel was in the office the day that Jim quit and wasn't sure if she was supposed to stay or follow him out the door. But stay she did, until her retirement in 1984 after 22 years of service.

Their children had specific chores around the house. Similar to a military muster, Jim lined them up in birth order each morning and barked out orders for the day; each child peeled off after receiving assignments. Sometimes he committed them to outside jobs, such as serving as janitors at Salem Baptist Church. Each Saturday morning his children walked to church to dust, sweep, clean toilets, mop and wax floors in preparation for services the next morning. On one occasion, a ram from Jim's farm broke through a glass window panel beside the door and made a mess in the church. His children begged their dad to let them quit after that cleaning chore, but to no avail.

Jim Wehmer, following his annual tradition of reading the Christmas story from the Bible after putting up their tree, 1955. Around him clockwise from top, Jack, Ruth, Bob, Gay, Jill and Jim. Six more children were yet to come.

Jim was a strict disciplinarian, and his children knew never to talk back to him. Only Lisa, who has Down Syndrome, could get away with it. When she was about five, Lisa sat unnoticed under an open kitchen countertop while Jim was lambasting some of his sons for not doing their chores. In the midst of his lengthy harangue a hidden voice spoke up, "Oh, just shut up, Dad!" Jim had to turn away so his children would not see him laughing at Lisa's audacity.

During summer 1958, Jack accidentally caught the hay barn on fire while Jim and Hazel were at son Jim's baseball game. The children at home, with Ruth babysitting, ran down their long driveway to escape the flames, which engulfed their barn and headed toward the house. They made a quick trip back after realizing one of the four-month-old twins, Louie or Lyle, remained at home in his crib. Word got to Jim that his house was on fire, and he came racing home. When he arrived and saw that it was the barn, which by then had burned to the ground, his great relief resulted in a hastily called party for the entire ball team. Everyone roasted hot dogs and marshmallows over the embers, and Hazel served apple cobbler and ice cream.

The fire wasn't Jack's only near-death experience. Not long before he started first grade, Jack and some siblings were playing on the back of Jim's wheat drill as he changed fields. Jack's denim jacket caught in a gear, pulling his arm into the machinery. After getting help to release Jack's arm, Jim rushed him to the hospital. He had extensive surgery to repair his arm, nearly severed at the wrist, including skin grafts taken from his stomach and leg.

Bob also underwent extensive hospitalization during childhood. After waking up one morning unable to walk, doctors diagnosed him with osteomyelitis, an infection in the bone marrow. Shortly after being released, Bob broke brittle bones in both legs while running through a field. The injury required a full plaster body cast on both legs and up to his chest. There were other mishaps as well in this family. Jeff fell off a horse at age 11 and had his arm in traction for a week, then crashed a motorcycle at age 12 requiring stitches in his head and neck. Greg flipped a truck three times on black ice* and walked away. But for the most part their accidents stemmed from rough and tumble activities 12 kids could get into growing up on a farm. Two middle children, Gay and Jean, insisted on doing everything the "big kids" did, and their toughness resulted in nicknames, "Nails" and "Little Nails." One day while swinging across the creek on grapevines, Jean lost her grip and dropped into the creek below, breaking her right elbow. But she refused to cry.

All the Wehmer children took after their parents in high school and into college, with

---

* Black ice is a coating of glazed ice on a surface such as a road. The ice itself is not black, but visually transparent, allowing the road below to be seen through it. This ice is typically invisible to drivers or people walking on it, thus causing accidents.

The Wehmer family and their kin have had a long relationship with the University of Missouri. In 1839 Zadok Riggs, third great grandfather of Hazel Snoddy Wehmer, joined Boone County residents in contributing funds to establish the university in Columbia. Above, columns from the original Academic Building, destroyed by fire in 1892, remain a symbol linking the university to its history. (© Bill Bachmann / Alamy Stock Photo)

some being athletic like their father and others studious like their mother. All seven Wehmer boys participated in high school Varsity sports, and Jill served as captain of the University of Missouri women's basketball team at a time when Title IX regulations were being put into place.* Beyond athletics, Wehmer children held leadership positions in their large classes. Ruth gave the salutatorian address at her high school commencement in 1965, but Hazel could not attend. She was in the hospital having the last Wehmer baby. As Ruth's graduation present, she received the honor of naming

him: Gregory Paul. Ruth and Gay followed their mother to Christian College and Ruth, Jill and Jean, along with numerous grandchildren, graduated from the University of Missouri. Other Wehmer children went to various colleges and universities across the state.

Actively involved in his children's lives, Jim also played leadership roles in the community and Salem Baptist Church. He served on Hazelwood School District's board for nine years, including the last three as president. During that time he helped oversee the merger of 13 smaller rural schools into a district

---

* *Title IX is a landmark federal civil rights law prohibiting sex-based discrimination in any school or education program that receives funding from the federal government, including equal rights in athletic programs.*

covering 78 square miles, an area larger than the City of St. Louis.[14] Jim died of a heart attack in 1978 at age 59, but diabetes also compromised his health, resulting in one leg being amputated. Typical of his stubbornness and independence, he grew impatient waiting for a prosthetic leg and carved his own peg leg from a block of wood. He didn't let on to doctors that he was walking long before getting medical clearance. After finally getting his "official" leg, his doctor was astonished when he immediately took off across the room.

Hazel continued raising their large family of kids, spoiling grandkids and carrying on family traditions until her death in 1995 at age 73. When Hazel's health began to fail, Gay moved back into the family home to care for her, along with Lisa, and continues as primary caregiver for Lisa. Hazel fought a long battle with cancer, strokes and other illnesses, but she remained feisty to the end. She never really gave up smoking, and after her marriage Hazel lit cigarettes outside, away from her disapproving husband. When chided by her children for smoking during a hospital stay, she reminded everyone, "I have rectal cancer, not lung cancer, so mind your own business."[15] Hazel's many life experiences led to one trait that stayed with her to the grave. She could talk and empathize with anyone and treated everyone the same, prince or pauper.

Unfortunately, many of their descendants never knew Jim or Hazel, yet they were bigger than life to their children and shaped who they became. This essay does not go beyond Jim and Hazel, other than recognition of their seven sons and five daughters. It remains to each of their children to carry their stories down to the next generations. Jim and Hazel lived lives filled with sacrifice, hard work and love. And they were the better for it. So are their children.

The Jim and Hazel Wehmer children celebrating Hazel's 70th birthday, 1992. Back row from left, Greg, Jack, Jim, Bob, Louie, Lyle, Jeff; front row from left, Jill, Gay, Hazel, Lisa, Jean, Ruth.

James and Hazel Wehmer Family

Married
25 Nov 1944
Florissant, MO

James Henry Wehmer
b. 26 Mar 1919
d. 10 Sep 1978

Hazel Marie Snoddy
b. 25 Mar 1922
d. 2 Sep 1995

Children

James Alan "Jim"
b. 19 Mar 1946
sp. Mary Ellen Lohman
Kammerer
d. 29 Jul 2014

**"Ruth" Anne
(Hawkins)**
b. 31 Mar 1947
sp. Van Hawkins

John Clifford "Jack"
b. 6 Aug 1949
sp. Susan Ellsworth

Robert Dennis "Bob"
b. 15 Jun 1951
sp. Dani Lynn Newfeld
d. 24 Jan 2005

Mary "Jill"
b. 18 Dec 1952
sp. Jane Small

**Margaret
"Gay" (Cusumano)**
b. 21 Aug 1954

Rilla "Jean" (Bozoian)
b. 2 Nov 1956
sp. Steve Bozoian

**Samuel Louis
"Louie"**
b. 3 Apr 1958

Steven "Lyle"
b. 3 Apr 1958
sp. Laura Rosner

Jeffrey Scott "Jeff"
b. 15 Dec 1959

"Lisa" Kay
b. 30 Jul 1961

Gregory Paul "Greg"
b. 1 Jun 1965
sp. Lynda Frohock

End Notes

[1] *TWA Skyliner Magazine* (Kansas City: Transcontinental and Western Air, Inc., 1943-1944), vol. 7-8 (Digital.shsmo.org).

[2] Robert Sherrod, *History of Marine Corps Aviation in World War II* (Washington: Combat Forces Press, 1952), 162.

[3] 1944 March 20-22 entries, "VMF(N) 531 – War Diary, 3/1/44 to 5/31/44 (ACA Reports, 52)," National Archives.

[4] May Summary, "VMF(N) 531 – War Diary, 3/1/44 to 5/31/44 (ACA Reports, 52)," National Archives.

[5] June Summary, "VMF(N) 531 – War Diary, 6/1/44 to 6/31/44 (ACA Reports, 52)," National Archives.

[6] 30 Mar 1944 letter, James H. Wehmer to Hazel Wagner (cousin), Family Collection.

[7] 29 Mar 1944 letter, James H. Wehmer to Hazel Wagner (cousin), Family Collection.

[8] "History, World War II," *Welcome to the Gray Ghosts Squadron* (531grayghostsquadron.org).

[9] Charles J. Quilter II and John C. Chapin, *A History of Marine Fighter Attack Squadron 531* (Washington D.C.: History and Museums Division, U.S. Marine Corp, 2001), 19.

[10] Air Medal Award, case of Capt. James H. Wehmer, USMCR, Commandant of Marine Corps, Headquarters U.S. Marine Corps, Washington, DC, 24 Apr 1950.

[11] James H. Wehmer, Marine Corps Report of Separation, 28 Dec. 1945, Eagle Mountain Lake, TX, Family Collection.

[12] "Checking Erosion, A St. Louis County Farm is Terraced So Excess Water May Be Controlled," *St. Louis Post Dispatch,* 20 Jul 1947, 5.

[13] "Marine Flyer a Full-Time Farmer," *St. Louis Star-Times,* 18 Jul 1949, 19.

[14] Gregory M. Franzwa, *History of the Hazelwood School District* (Florissant, MO: Board of Education, 1977), 1.

[15] Conversations with family, August 1995.

About the Author

Ruth Hawkins grew up in Florissant, Missouri, and resides in Jonesboro, Arkansas. During her career, she has been a television reporter, newspaper feature writer and public school information officer in Tidewater, Virginia. She served as a higher education administrator in various capacities at Arkansas State University for more than 40 years before her retirement in 2019.

Ruth is the author of *Unbelievable Happiness and Final Sorrow: The Hemingway-Pfeiffer Marriage*, which is a biographical work on author Ernest Hemingway's relationship with the Pfeiffer family of Piggott, Arkansas. The book is considered a landmark study on Pauline Pfeiffer and her influence on Hemingway's life and work.

She is an inductee into the Arkansas Women's Hall of Fame and recipient of numerous state and national heritage tourism and preservation awards. Ruth also has certifications in American Records and methodology through the International Institute of Genealogical Studies.

She holds undergraduate degrees from Christian College (now Columbia College) and the University of Missouri School of Journalism, a master's degree from Arkansas State University and a doctorate from the University of Mississippi.

Ruth and her husband Van have a son and daughter-in-law, Curt Hawkins and Amy Schmidt, who also live in Jonesboro.

www.ingramcontent.com/pod-product-compliance
Lightning Source LLC
Chambersburg PA
CBHW061135030426
42334CB00003B/50